SCOTTISH SEASIDE TOWNS

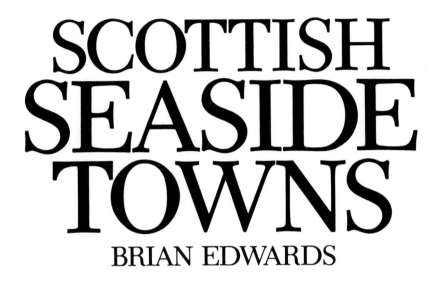

SCOTTISH SEASIDE TOWNS

BRIAN EDWARDS

Photographs by Ken MacGregor

BRITISH BROADCASTING CORPORATION

For Ben and Alice Poppy

Published by the British Broadcasting Corporation
35 Marylebone High Street London W1M 4AA

First published 1986
© Brian Edwards 1986
ISBN 0 563 20452 4

Set in 9 on 11pt Photina and
Printed in Great Britain by Butler & Tanner Ltd, Frome, Somerset

CONTENTS

Preface   7

Introduction   9

St Andrews   13

Kirkwall   33

Crail   51

Kirkcudbright   69

Inveraray   89

Rothesay   107

Index   126

PREFACE

As an Englishman living in Scotland I always felt that Scottish towns were noticeably different from those south of the border. It was not just that they looked different but they felt different, their whole character was quite alien to the urban traditions I had grown up with. This uniqueness was part of the fun of exploring Scottish towns and I soon discovered that some of the best and least spoilt of the towns were by the sea.

The uniqueness of Scottish towns and their buildings is one of the issues I have sought to highlight in this book. In an age when tower blocks look the same in Glasgow and Paris, and new houses are identical in Aberdeen and Southampton, it seems important to hang on to our traditions. Scotland's towns are different from those elsewhere for very good reasons. Her climate is more severe than in most of Europe, her supply of building stone is second to none and her property law is almost unique.

Just as the Scottish landscape is special and distinctive, so are the towns.

By the sea the climate is more extreme, the regional traditions better preserved, and the sense of history more visible, and so the television programmes and book have focused upon Scottish seaside towns. But the same principles of building and pattern of development apply elsewhere in Scotland.

In pursuing this path of discovery my thanks must go principally to Ken MacGregor, the director of the BBC television series, who shared my enthusiasm and steered the idea through countless committees; also to Keith Alexander, the series producer, whose gentle guidance was always appreciated. And to Annette Rogers, the production assistant, whose patience and tact calmed many a tense moment, to Theresa Lenaghan who typed the manuscript, and Bill Lindsay who prepared the town maps.

INTRODUCTION

Is there such a thing as a Scottish seaside tradition? Do Scotland's towns have a unique urban dimension, different from that south of the border or across the North Sea? The answer to both questions is probably yes but to varying degrees.

Communication has always been a problem for Scotland. A wild and largely inaccessible rural hinterland has forced the nation's towns onto the fertile coastal strip or a few well-sheltered river valleys. Water was the chief means of movement, and the only one for goods. Towns became established alongside navigable water, and that generally meant the sea. There arose a pattern of coastal towns, a tradition of seaside architecture, quite distinctive from that of most of Britain. This book seeks to explore that tradition by taking a close look at six Scottish towns – St Andrews, Kirkwall, Crail, Kirkcudbright, Inveraray and Rothesay.

Life by the sea is influenced more by climate than that inland. Buildings and urban spaces are shaped as much by the forces of nature as by the dictates of function or taste. A tradition grows up, gradually over time, where only the best survive and this becomes part of the way of doing things. Hence a pattern of building evolves where gables are thrust into the wind, where windows are never large and deeply set into thick walls, and where outside spaces are small and sheltered.

You could call it a Scottish tradition, and it certainly becomes so when buildings are piled up high upon each other to form the characteristic tenemental scene of many ancient burghs. But by the sea, the harsh elements prevent too much high building and here expansion, when it occurs, tends to be infilling of open spaces within the town. Gradually spaces become smaller and more precious, ending up with an arrangement as in Kirkwall in Orkney, where buildings are jammed together like the pattern on a Fair Isle jumper. In fact, the further north you go, the denser the old towns become, producing a closely-grained form of urban development quite unlike the more spacious towns of the south.

In northern Scotland, climate is the dominant factor which shapes people's lives. Their buildings, their boats, their faces, their landscapes, all bear witness to the powerful forces of nature. Even the people of the Iron Age had the good sense to build partly underground and, when their structures were above ground, to build robust circular brochs, providing the least resistance to a perpetual wind. Further south, climate, function and form continue to be closely associated but here one can detect other influences. Some are directly the result of cultural contacts made in an expanding medieval world of trade and commerce. There is likely to be a market square, tolbooth or harbour, each planned and built with considerable care by an emerging burgess class. Where trading links had been forged across the North Sea, there may be Dutch inspiration, for example in the design of the public buildings in Crail or the private houses in St Andrews.

Somewhat later, the concern for amenity and landscape, introduced in the eighteenth century, finds its expression in a formally planned square or in woodland planting around the town. In towns such as Inveraray, town planning takes on a special significance and the result is a marvellous fusion of the work of man and of nature. In other towns, an older settlement is greatly enhanced by the addition of a new town grafted onto the earlier streets. Kirkcudbright is a good example.

Occasionally, the nineteenth century has left its mark with a baronial town hall or a daring bridge of iron construction. In Rothesay, the Victorians went further and created a seaside resort of Winter Gardens and handsome terraces of tenements around the ancient castle. In most of our seaside towns, there were harbour improvements to strengthen the work of unnamed medieval masons. Great Scottish engineers of the nineteenth century, like Thomas Telford or Robert Stevenson, may well have had a hand in their construction, working perhaps for the British Fisheries Society.

Whatever the work and whenever the period, life by the sea demands attention to detail and to design. There are no short cuts when storms threaten to uncover a poorly laid harbour wall or a shoddily constructed gable end. The Scottish tradition is always to be found where materials – usually stone in various guises – is combined with honest craftsmanship to produce the towns we cherish today.

Scotland is exceptionally fortunate in her supply of natural stones. For century upon century, stone was the accepted form of building. The Vikings had to bring master masons from Durham to the northern isles to help build Kirkwall's St Magnus Cathedral, finding no timber in Orkney on which to apply their carpentry skills. Scottish stone is exploited in every area; grey granite in Aberdeenshire, red sandstone in Dumfriesshire and East Lothian, yellow sandstone in Edinburgh and Glasgow, pink stone in Perthshire and even green stone in Angus. Stone was the great urban unifier, producing countless cliffs of streets in granite or sandstone.

Walls in Scotland are left as natural stone or harled – a protective render of lime and sand, which can be coloured. Stone walls are finished in a variety of ways, sometimes by elaborate tooling of the surface. Roofs tend to be finished in flagstone, clay pantile or most frequently slate. Slate is as great a unifier of Scottish roofscapes as stone is for walls and together they make up a fine tradition of building, perfectly equipped to withstand a harsh climate.

Status is expressed with a carved lintel here, a moulded door surround there, or perhaps by a decorated skew-putt (the lowest stone on the crow-step). Later, classical columns may appear, even a portico, but these imported elements of style never quite dominated the indigenous Scottish manner of building. It was a pattern of building which endured in Scotland well into the twentieth century, and, in fact, its very traditional qualities were exploited by some of her greatest recent architects. Charles Rennie Mackintosh and Robert Lorimer both built in the Scottish manner and praised the timeless qualities of this form of building. But the internationalism of building which came with the Modern Movement in the 1930s broke what had been a continuous wave of urban development stretching back a thousand years. Concrete and brick then replaced stone, the flat roof replaced the pitched, the plate-glass window replaced the small-paned sash.

In certain Scottish cities, such as Kirkcaldy, a townscape of densely-packed buildings became, in less than a generation, an urban landscape of tower blocks. What had been close-grained and tightly packed became open and windswept. The bond between built form, urban tradition and climate was broken, particularly in the major towns.

In our coastal towns, the pressures for change and keeping up with urban fashions were less marked. Here the local builders knew that a style of building imported from southern France or Germany with its wafer-thin walls and windows pushed out to the wallface was hardly likely to survive the force of an Atlantic gale for long. So sense prevailed and in time the conservation movement ensured the survival of at least the best examples of Scottish seaside towns. Local preservation societies took the lead, as at St Andrews, saving whole stretches of streets when they looked under threat of demolition.

Tourism too has had a positive effect, bringing to the old towns jobs and money which could then be used to repair a roof or justify the saving of an ancient building from demolition. The picture postcard has always focused on an attractive harbourside view and soon town councils were anxious to play their part, if only because of the tourist revenue which could be earned. But there are problems: tourists can demand 'historic' images which a town has never possessed, and pampering to their tastes by creating pseudo-Scottish scenes for the camera lens undermines the integrity of old towns.

The survival of our old buildings and in some senses even whole towns depends increasingly upon adapting them to new uses. What was once a thriving fishing or trading town may now be a holiday centre, what was once a warehouse may now be flats or a craft workshop. Society is always creating new uses and somehow these have to be directed towards empty historic buildings. Without a use an old building decays like a withered limb. Use is the key to survival. Fitting new uses into old shells is part of the character of ancient towns – part of the layering of history which extends beyond architecture into social change. All of our six towns have provided examples of survival through change of function as against change of building. It saves on resources and helps to preserve character and continuity.

Form, function and climate are closely interwoven in our six towns. Stone, the skill of the craftsman, the vision of the designer are all essential ingredients. From the Viking north to the soft landscapes of the south-west, Scotland has a priceless and enjoyable heritage of old towns. Caring and conserving involves us all, not just the professional architect or town planner. This heritage is Scotland's memory built in stone.

Towns are our greatest cultural achievement. They represent the biggest concentration of art and design in our world. Everything around us is designed – the buildings, the cars, the lamp standards, the clothes people wear. Inside the buildings the interiors are designed; the furniture and the paintings that hang on the wall have been shaped by an artist. Although their presence is not always that obvious designers and artists crop up everywhere. Towns have been shaped by them over the centuries and continue to be so.

This book, and the programmes on which they are based, seeks to explore the visual world of six seaside towns. By taking pleasure in the environment around us, our appreciation and awareness of the beauty and uniqueness of Scottish building grows. My task as writer and presenter of the series has been to share an enthusiasm for Scottish towns with the hope that what is different and precious about them will be preserved and enjoyed by others.

Aerial view of St Andrews

ST ANDREWS

First impressions of the character of a town, like that of a person, can usually be trusted. The prospect from afar when the town is still just a silhouette against a backcloth of hills or sea tells you a great deal about the place. Its skyline can be read and interpreted with as much assurance as the archaeologist reading some long-lost foundations.

St Andrews has a sharp skyline where the conspicuous church towers or spires still perform their ancient symbolic role. Public buildings, be they ecclesiastical or secular, have always enjoyed special emphasis in the skyline of historic towns. In St Andrews the tall square tower of St Rule's church sits prominently at the seaward end of the town surrounded by the craggy remains of what was once Scotland's largest cathedral. A little inland, the church towers of St Salvator's College and Holy Trinity provide just enough counterbalance to a skyline which is never disappointing no matter which direction you approach it from.

The skyline of St Andrews has changed little over the past three hundred years. In 1690, it was recorded by the Dutch artist John Slezer and the town looks much the same today. Then and now topography, architecture, seascape and landscape are fused to create an immediately recognisable historic town of learning and religion. What has changed most is not the town but the surrounding landscape. Golf courses and enclosed barley fields now replace the open medieval strips.

Clear skylines usually mean attractive towns, confused skylines tend to reflect disjointed towns. The planners' role is never easy when seeking to preserve skyline in the face of commercial pressure. Edinburgh has just managed to save one of the best city skylines in Europe, in stark contrast to Glasgow whose skyline outside the Victorian centre is as confusing as any. In this aspect the two cities are worlds apart. St Andrews is not, of course, under the same developmental pressure, but its skyline needs careful handling, for even a small office block can do great harm to many cherished views.

The skyline of St Andrews is perhaps best seen from approach roads on the south where the towers are set as silhouettes against the wide expanse of the North Sea. Upon entering the town these distant landmarks become more immediate point references for orientation – clues to the spatial relationships of the place. Soon the network of streets and alleyways, at first difficult to comprehend and tantalisingly similar in character, can be arranged into a rough mental map with the help of the landmarks. These early stages in the discovery of a town are sometimes the most enjoyable, when being lost can involve marvellous new discoveries. St Andrews is this sort of town – a patchwork of streets, wynds and squares inviting exploration. But it is different from the other towns in this book. It is essentially a spiritual and academic centre and although it has enjoyed a certain secular distinction as a trading town and the home of golf, markets and commerce have always taken a bit of a back seat.

St Andrews is a good example of a planned medieval burgh. It is as planned, in its own rather casual way, as the new towns of the eighteenth or twentieth century. The town represents planning in the fashion of the Middle Ages, before the age of the tee square, set square or even the discovery of geometric

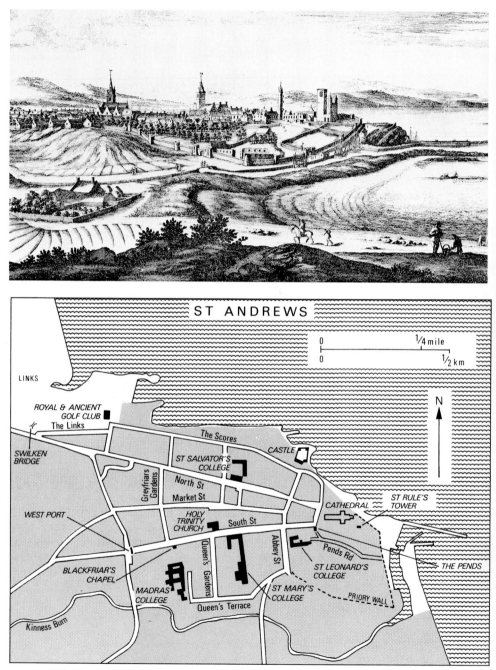

Top: John Slezer's view of St Andrews, 1690

perspective. The planned town consists of two roughly parallel streets, North Street and South Street, converging upon the Cathedral. Between them but not penetrating to the ecclesiastical environs of the Cathedral, runs Market Street whose name describes its original function. All three streets are the result of conscious planning, when deliberate decisions were required to accommodate growth following the conferment of its burgh status in the twelfth century. The town planning may have the gentle naïvety of a medieval painting but the bishop's plan exploits the coastal plateau with uncanny assurance.

Unlike most medieval settlements in Scotland, St Andrews was a bishop's town. It was an episcopal burgh founded in 1140 by the ruling clergy. The function of the town was to generate an income to help support the religious house nearby. St Andrews ceased to be an ecclesiastical burgh of barony, as these religious urban settlements were called, at the

Reformation when James VI made the town into a Royal Burgh. The twelfth century provided St Andrews with a planned, if rather sketchy, framework for future growth. It took centuries to expand the plan, and achieve the continuous blocks of development we see today, but the original concept of principal streets focusing upon the Cathedral has served St Andrews well.

In European terms there are two types of medieval town – those that were consciously planned (for defence, trade or religious foundations) and those which grew organically. Most of the Scottish towns of the Middle Ages fit into the first group and of these, St Andrews is a particularly good example of a town planned by the clergy.

The two principal streets – North Street and South Street – run roughly east west. They focus on the Cathedral at the seaward end and at the landward end are protected by gateways or ports. Around the town there once ran a

West Port, rebuilt in 1589, with South Street through arch

burgh wall whose function was both defensive and administrative. As defensive structures burgh walls provided some protection but their main function was to control the movement of goods and people – to secure the taxes and tolls that paid for the running of the town as well as the King's army and royal palaces.

West Port, rebuilt in 1589 on the site of an older gateway, is the best surviving medieval town gateway in Scotland. Although much restored and altered (the two side arches are Victorian modifications) it has, with its twinned octagonal towers and gun-loops along the parapet, an air of serious fortification which perhaps exaggerates its real function. Few other urban gateways in Scotland are as well preserved although a similar-looking entranceway to Linlithgow Palace survives and a copy of this, built to a reduced size, decorates the driveway to Sir Walter Scott's Abbotsford, near Melrose. West Port may still exist but sadly its immediate environment is greatly marred by petrol filling stations.

An extensive length of medieval wall still surrounds the precincts of the Priory and Cathedral. These defensive walls, considered some of the best ecclesiastical fortifications in Europe, enclose an area of thirty acres and extend for over a mile. Their original purpose was to provide security for a great Anglo-Norman priory, whose monastic buildings south of the cathedral church included extensive cloisters and the usual collection of subsidiary buildings like brew houses. These priory walls, known locally as the Abbey Walls, give a good impression of how burgh walls would have looked. Tall (they average twenty feet in height) and sturdy, the wall has thirteen towers, one of which was rebuilt in 1971 to allow a realignment of the road. When several of the round towers and their linking walls can be seen together, as in The Shore, they provide a wonderful edge to the historic core of St Andrews.

Like the West Port in the burgh wall, the entrance gateway to the priory grounds is a rather grand and elaborate affair. Known as The Pends it predates the West Port by at least two centuries. The roof and upper storey of The Pends were removed, probably at the Reformation, but the decorated pointed arches and the springers for the gothic vaulting still exist to indicate the former magnificence of this entranceway. It was here that pilgrims and merchants once waited whilst their credentials were checked in what was a splendid border post between two distinct worlds. St Andrews was, for centuries, a town within a town. One town was the huge monastic settlement, the Canterbury of Scotland, and the other, the secular and academic town.

The monastery with its large cathedral church, second in length in Britain to Norwich, sits in a most unlikely place. Placed almost on the headlands above the harbour and Kinness Burn, the site has always been exposed to the elements. The siting of the cathedral here, partly for defensive reasons and partly because the pre-Norman church of St Rule was already well established, has had its problems. Winter gales have always brought periodic havoc to the east coast of Scotland. Cathedral records show that the ancient church suffered much in storms – for example, the west end was destroyed in 1275, the south transept in 1409. But the present shipwreck of a cathedral, a mere ghost of its former glory, is the result of destruction by protestants at the Reformation and subsequent plundering of the ancient stones for building purposes. It was a majestic building by any standards, built to impress and to last. Looking at the wreck of the Cathedral today, one cannot help feeling sad. Like a stranded whale on the beach this once beautiful and dignified building stands broken, a mere picturesque graveyard for the tourists.

Re-using the stones of older buildings was a common practice in Scotland throughout the Middle Ages and extended even into the nineteenth century. Often the ancient stones were used for semi-official purposes and enjoyed the

The Pends: the fourteenth-century gateway to the Priory

sanction of local leaders. In St Andrews, some of the old college walls and burgess gardens incorporate stones from earlier buildings. The harbour, rebuilt frequently from 1559 onwards, is known to have used stones from the castle. We may condemn such practices as vandalism today, but for the poorly housed Scot, it was natural resourcefulness.

St Rule's tower which stands nearby affords splendid views of the town. Legend has assigned the Greek monk St Regulus or Rule to having stolen relics of the apostle St Andrew and taken them to Scotland in the fourth century for safe-keeping. He was apparently shipwrecked here, and a religious house was founded around the relics, consisting, it is said, of St Andrew's arm-bone, three fingers, a tooth and knee-cap! Such picturesque legends are the substance of much Scottish history.

The church and tower of St Rule clearly predate the Norman Conquest. The tall square tower and narrow round headed windows re-call indigenous Scottish practice before the imposition of the rather standardised architecture of the Normans. Notice how on the chapel side of the tower, three different roof pitches have existed in the building's long history. Notice too how this solid, small windowed church has survived the battering of countless storms far better than the more elaborate cathedral.

The security of the priory walls was not sufficient for the senior clergy who built themselves a courtyard castle on the clifftop known as the Episcopal Palace or Bishop's Castle. The Middle Ages were difficult times for bishops, as for other landowners, and defence of the body was nearly as important to senior clergy as elevation of the soul.

The Bishop's Castle was founded in 1200 but most of the surviving buildings date from the fifteenth century. Looking at the construction, it is obvious that the castle was built for passive defence rather than outward aggression. Despite the sprinkling of gun-loops and guarded entrance doorway, the castle was really an inward-looking palace of relative convenience for comfort-seeking bishops.

Religion and politics can make a hateful combination and the ruined castle was the scene of many horrors in the name of God. It was here many early religious reformers were held and burnt to death or left to rot in the darkness of the bottle dungeon. The castle's history is closely linked with the early days of the Reformation, of siege and counter-siege, and the ghostly subterranean passages date from this time. But the castle was once a building of relative comfort where kitchens and fine apartments lit by oriel windows ensured that the ruling clergy at least could escape the frugality of monastic life.

When you move inland through the town, you move forwards through time. As you journey from east to west – from the Cathedral on the headlands to the Victorian terraces that line the links – your path is charting a route through St Andrews' history. Between the ancient and lost town of the bishops and the golfing town of the eighteenth and nineteenth centuries, there is one important link – the university town.

The bishops not only shaped St Andrews by their town planning, they also made the town a centre of learning. Bishop Wardlaw established the university in 1412, making it the first in Scotland. Like the universities of Oxford and Cambridge, St Andrews was based upon a college system, with each college having its own principal and staff of professors. As a consequence, each college had its own architecture, and its own collection of teaching and residential buildings. Colleges were fairly self-contained and arranged around courtyards which were often approached from the main streets via entrance gateways. These medieval colleges create, uniquely in Scotland, a townscape not only of streets but of courtyards and connecting alleyways. The enclosed courtyard set apart from the public streets becomes a vital element in the tapestry of urban spaces which make up the town.

There are three principal collections of college buildings: St Salvator's, established in 1450, St Leonard's in 1512 and St Mary's in 1537. Together with their supporting coffee houses and bookshops, the colleges give St Andrews the leisured air of a university town.

Of the colleges, St Salvator's is the largest and best represents the architecture of learning. It was founded by Bishop Kennedy, grandson of Robert III, and former Chancellor of Scotland who was described in his time as 'wondrous godile and wise, weill learned in divine services, and in the civill lawis'. Although the original buildings have mostly gone, save the college church, their successors, arranged around connecting quadrangles, evoke the mood of former days. The courtyards and quadrangles, mostly set out as lawns with a few handsome old trees, have provided a good environment for some attractive buildings, many dating from the nineteenth century. Into this landscape has also been placed a modern concrete and glass library which serves the whole university. The rather harsh lines of the library may horrify some observers, and the horizontal banding of the building seems to me to pay scant regard to the character of the older neighbours. Yet taste in architecture, which is, after all, the most public of the arts, changes fast and time remains the best judge of what is good. On the credit side the library, by its careful siting, creates yet further courtyards of space between itself and its neighbours, and carefully preserves a fine sycamore tree.

The college church of St Salvator's provides a much-needed vertical point reference along the wide and lengthy North Street. Positioned right on the building line of the rest of the street, the tall tower and stone spire are symbolic of their function, when learning and religion meant much the same thing. This late medieval church is unusually intact and contains the pulpit from which John Knox preached. In this pulpit, a contemporary of Knox records that he would: 'Ding the pulpit to blads [bang it to bits] and fly out of it.' St Salvator's Chapel was never a town church, its function was related to the fairly self-contained world of the college.

St Salvator's College extends via connecting courtyards all the way from North Street to The Scores. The Scores, once known as Swallow Gait, is a street of ancient origin which is lined by some characteristically beautiful walls, part of which incorporate a corbelled turret, once a

Above: the modern university library behind North Street. Left: the College Church of St Salvator's from North Street

19

feature of Swallow Port. The enclosure of streets and lanes by high stone walls is a recurring feature of St Andrews and, when mixed with courts and quadrangles, can produce a townscape of considerable charm. It is a quality which is best explored on foot and at a leisurely pace, for the progression of events and succession of spaces are not to be hurried.

St Leonard's College was founded half a century after St Salvator's. At St Leonard's, we again have a courtyard of buildings, this time approached via an archway from Pends Road. The site is an ancient one lying close to the priory walls and was, before 1512, occupied by an ancient hospice run by Augustinian monks. Today, it is occupied by a girls' residential school which uses some of the old college buildings. The original college chapel, built in the early sixteenth century and recently restored by the university, is open to the public.

St Mary's College was founded in 1537 by Archbishop James Beaton whose nephew, Cardinal David Beaton, was killed nine years later by the protestant reformers and left to hang for all to see outside his apartment window in the Bishop's Castle. It has a long courtyard entered via an attractive gateway with the coats of arms of former chancellors over the arch and the Latin motto from St John's Gospel: 'In the beginning was the Word', an appropriate choice for a college. Here buildings and urban landscape are delightfully integrated; ancient buildings enclosing equally ancient trees. The thorn tree, well propped these days, is said to have been planted by Mary, Queen of Scots. Looking almost as old, though less frail, is the splendid holm oak whose branches dip nearly down to the lawns.

Nearby there is a dovecot which would have provided much-needed winter meat for the academics, not to mention eggs in the spring, tender chicks in the summer and feathers for mattresses throughout the year. Not far away a sundial, dated 1664, once provided a useful measure of time for the benefit of both students and teachers. On St Mary's College Tower (to

the west of the gateway) the original lime and sea-shell pointing survives, producing a splendid silvery edging to the old stones. Some of the fragments of shells are almost as large as cornflakes.

The effect of the many courtyards and their connecting lanes and wynds is to create a world for the pedestrian away from the bustle and noise of the main streets. These more private parts of the town, semi-public rather than truly public, seem to invite contemplation and uninterrupted thought. They may be enclosed courtyards in an urban design sense, yet their

real purpose was probably to encourage journeys through the mind, where teachers and
student could explore Latin texts away from
the worldly street.

You can always tell a university town by the
bookshops and coffee houses. Tucked away in
back lanes or in converted warehouses or
churches, bookshops and cafés introduce a leisured air to a town. In St Andrews the book-
sellers J. and G. Innes, on the corner of Church
Street and South Street, provides the town
with a classic university bookshop. Not too
serious in its use of carved oak and diamond-

St Mary's College with holm oak, and stonework detail showing sea-shell pointing

Above: Market Street. Right: fisherman's cottage with characteristic forestair

leaded glazing, the shopfront incorporates the university arms amongst some jolly carving. Right on the corner there is a tiny oriel window placed like a sentry box above the street. This cheerful piece of shop design was built as recently as 1928.

The three principal streets of St Andrews – North Street, South Street and Market Street – are all exceptionally wide by medieval standards. Their width is not just a measure of the concern for amenity shown by the town-planning bishops. It also reflects the number of pilgrims that flooded into the town. The widest is South Street and the narrowest Market Street which, except for its swelling at the centre to form the market square, is the least dignified of the three. St Andrews was never a town wholly of commerce, and the civic importance attached to the two streets which serve the colleges reflects their elevated status at the expense of the marketplace. Today, shopping and commerce are concentrated in Market Street and the adjoining areas. Their relative congestion stands in contrast to the open, tree-lined and quieter North and South Streets.

The town of St Andrews has always played a large supporting part in the life of the university. In the very early days, the Cathedral was the town's biggest employer, today it is the university. Town and gown, college and street, have for centuries enjoyed a special relationship. But there was always a St Andrews which maintained an independent existence free of the patronage of the college. This was the trading town of wealthy burgesses and the fishing town of humbler stock. Both co-exist on the doorstep of the medieval Priory and colleges.

The width of North Street alongside St Salvator's Chapel, and of South Street throughout much of its length, seems somewhat out of proportion to the size of the enclosing buildings. At times, they feel more like linear

squares than actual streets. Their width gives ample space for tree-planting, although the sight of wide streets lined on both sides by trees is rather un-Scottish. The trees are mostly lime and wych elm, not the planes of London or Paris which would hardly survive this far north. We tend to associate trees with the countryside but in many parts of Britain, including Fife, we have to look to the towns for providing a leafy view.

The width of street has led also to the development of wide pavements and sometimes attractive areas of cobbles or setts. The dignity of these streets is somewhat undermined by lines of gaunt lamp standards whose height and position seem intent upon spoiling the view. These streets are surely the place for wall-mounted lights.

Looking eastwards along South Street, the view ends upon the toothy outline of the ruined cathedral. There is just enough curve in the street to relieve any sense of boredom and at two or three points tall towers or spires punctuate the vista. One of these is the Town Hall at the junction with Queen's Gardens, a building which in true Victorian fashion places its tower in such a position as to compete with Holy Trinity Church opposite. The Town Hall seeks rather self-consciously to decorate South Street, adding an air of baronial whimsy to this wide processional street. Tall and spiky, the Town Hall marks an important corner where a nineteenth-century street – Queen's Gardens – slices into medieval St Andrews.

On the side of the Town Hall there is a mosaic erected in 1941. It was designed and executed by Polish soldiers during the war to commemorate friendship between the two nations, following a stay by the Polish forces at Tentsmuir just north of the town. Art does much to brighten up a town and mosaics in particular have a long tradition of use in architecture.

Across the street Holy Trinity Church stands in a small square. It dates from 1410 and is said to occupy six half-length burgess strips with the more recent west front built on a seventh. Its position to the side of the street shows that the line of South Street had, by this early date, already been established. Holy Trinity is the parish church of St Andrews, as distinct from the collegiate churches or the monastic cathedral. The slightly subservient placing of the church suggests a strong control over the shaping of the town by the ruling bishops who were intent upon ensuring that all roads focused upon the cathedral, certainly not the town church.

Most of the Holy Trinity shows signs of heavy restoration. The worst damage was inflicted by the Georgian restorers who, in 1799, sought to remove all irregularities and hence much of the interest, though this was partly reversed by the scholarly architect MacGregor Chalmers in 1906. Today it is so restored, altered and re-restored that its value as an ancient building is practically nil although it still makes an important contribution to the street scene.

Further down South Street towards West Port, stands the fragmentary remains of Blackfriar's Chapel. It is all that remains of a once-extensive Dominican friary, established in 1274 and destroyed by the Reformation mob in 1559. This irregular construction was once part of the north transept of a handsome church. The history of St Andrews is written large in craggy ruins.

Behind it, set well back, stands Madras College, a fine range of buildings designed in the Jacobean style by William Burn of Edinburgh. The college was established in 1832, by bequest from a native of St Andrews, Andrew Bell, who made a fortune in India; hence the name. One regrets that the college is set so far back from the road allowing the sense of enclosure of the street to escape. Far better to have followed the usual pattern of college building in St Andrews – a courtyard entered from the main street by a gateway.

Much of South Street is lined by distinguished buildings, many built in the eighteenth century. The best stretch of unaltered and sometimes unassuming town houses is between St Mary's College and The Pends. Here there are several fine buildings, some mildly Dutch in appearance with their well-proportioned fronts and many-paned sash windows. There is little doubt that on the east coast the city architecture of Holland was one of the largest factors in shaping the character of Scottish towns in the seventeenth and eighteenth centuries.

Many of the buildings in South Street are older than the appearance of their front elevations would suggest. This is because, to an eighteenth-century man of taste, the quirks and irregularities of a medieval building were base. Great effort was made to disguise older buildings and present to the public a front elevation which had the love of proportion and stylistic unity the age demanded. They were, in effect, trying to 'keep up with the Joneses' or, in Scotland's case, the Adams. Behind these Georgian frontages we often find interiors incorporating such medieval features as painted ceilings, vaulted rooms and turnpike stairs.

In typical Scottish fashion, buildings on either side of South Street (with the exception of Madras College) form continuous cliffs of development without front gardens. It makes for a hard-edged urbanity more reminiscent of small continental towns than those in England. No two buildings are exactly the same, yet there is a consistency which unites the town.

This unity is achieved by the use of subtle rhythms which tie together buildings of different styles, materials or height. Rhythm presupposes a degree of pattern, and in the spacious and dignified South Street, it is achieved by three main means. There is a rhythm of colour, a rhythm of building height and a rhythm of building width.

Colour in architecture is the result of blending the natural colour of different building materials with applied colour. The range is mostly in the red to yellow band of the colour circle – colours which reflect the surrounding geology and the use of local stone. The redness of some sandstone is relieved by the use of grey harling or render and the redness of some clay pantiles by the use of grey slate. Sometimes different colour stones are used in the same building, perhaps as dressings to window surrounds or for quoins.

Sometimes colour is applied to stonework as well as timber, and the effect, as at Inveraray or Kirkcudbright, can be especially attractive when only margins or quoins are picked out. Taken together as a street scene, the colours of natural materials and judicious use of applied colour produces a kind of rhythm of colour which is quite distinct from a regular pattern of colour. Usually the rhythm has grown up rather accidentally but needs careful consideration today when a new building is slotted into an old street.

Rhythm is also established by the various heights of the buildings. In South Street (and elsewhere in St Andrews), buildings conform to a range between two and five storeys high with most either three or four storeys. The stepping up and down along the street of building rooflines, some with dormers and some without, some with gable ends to the street, produces a rhythm which complements that of the use of colour. These subtleties have evolved over three or four centuries as buildings have responded to different social needs, yet few buildings have seriously broken the unwritten rules.

The width of buildings also creates a rhythm. Few buildings are more than about forty feet wide and none less than fifteen, these widths being based originally upon the burgess strips or 'rigs' as they were known. Often wide rigs have become subdivided sometime in the past, but the tendency today is to buy up several adjoining houses and redevelop the whole site. This destroys the rhythm of the street as surely as buildings that are too high, or even too low.

When a large site is redeveloped as a single building, both rhythm and scale are difficult to keep within the range established elsewhere. In St Andrews, the 'Boots' development alongside the parish church seeks to overcome this problem by creating the impression that the shop is a number of different buildings standing side by side. Elsewhere, as in North Street, modern architects have sought to break an over-large façade into a number of separate parts each with its own identity. Some purists may question the morality of designing in this fashion but it can surely be justified if your interests lie in the town as against the individual building.

Traditionally, public buildings have enjoyed the right to break the codes of conduct which applied to private buildings. The church, the college, the town hall have all exercised a certain privilege in the town scene of St Andrews. These buildings are often positioned prominently (perhaps not so the parish church) and given spires or towers to signify their importance. The visual coding by spire and tower, or by façade, sets these buildings apart from the everyday architecture of the town. The problem for the planner today is to ensure that supermarket or office block does not assume the rights of a public building.

These general rules of conservation and urban design have, on the whole, been followed in St Andrews. There are a few exceptions but, thanks to some good fortune, a low level of economic activity and the fact that the town's two growth areas – the university and golf – have concentrated their building efforts outside the historic centre, the town survives intact.

Few towns in Scotland exhibit so clearly the medieval pattern of land rigs as St Andrews. Building plots are long and narrow, the front to the street being occupied by the burgess's house and the rear garden enclosed by a high stone wall. Ownership of these handsome walls is indicated by small recesses set in on the owner's side. Sometimes in the rear gardens we find a dovecot or a gazebo – a kind of summerhouse, often in some bizarre style.

Access to back lands or common grazing is frequently via narrow lanes or pends entered through an arched opening in the street. These lanes, or wynds as they are often known, become a familiar feature in the character of the town.

Often enclosed by high stone walls, lined sometimes by more recent building (mostly eighteenth or nineteenth century), the wynds become a third important element in the network of open spaces in St Andrews. After the spacious street and the peace and tranquillity of the quadrangle we have the intimacy of the wynd. Frequently wynds or back lanes are occupied by cottages or workshops but the tendency, especially around the market square, is for these to become secondary shopping streets. Here the pedestrian scale of the wynds lends itself to development as specialist shopping or café areas where quality of environment counts for more than speed of service.

Although St Andrews is a historic town by the sea, one is hardly aware of the presence of the water from much of the town. Unlike the Victorian resort of Rothesay, the town seems to turn its back on the sea. It is, in essence, an inward-looking town sheltered by countless high stone walls. Only at the cathedral or castle end of the town, or perhaps near the links, is the observer fully aware of the expanse of the North Sea.

The St Andrews Preservation Trust is one of the oldest in Scotland. It was founded in 1937 in the days when the conservation of old buildings, let alone whole towns, was far from fashionable. Local initiative can work wonders, especially when it is backed by a well-informed community and a little money. This preservation society has restored a number of old buildings, usually on a revolving fund basis, when buildings are bought, restored and sold again with profits going into new projects. By such means, this and other societies, including the National Trust for Scotland, have carried the burden of conservation which

Louden's Close

should really have been the responsibility of local authorities. Yet it is a sad fact of Scottish life that in countless small towns, buildings which had stood for centuries have been needlessly demolished in the past thirty years.

Of the many buildings restored by the St Andrews Preservation Trust, that at 12 North Street is both a house and a local museum, with an excellent photographic archive. Built in the eighteenth century, it is made of red sandstone, much decayed in parts, beneath a pantiled roof. The pantiles would most probably have been made in Holland, since Fife had no tile works at this early date. Pantiles are a common feature of St Andrews and are usually set between crow-stepped gables. Sometimes the side laps are pointed with mortar to prevent driving snow from penetrating into the roof space and, occasionally, the lower courses are finished in slate, as can be seen at Shore Mill by the harbour.

A roof finished in pantiles is normally a simple rectangular affair. The large folded tiles do not lend themselves to complex roof forms and where dormers break into pantiled roofs they are normally finished in slate. Sometimes pantiles replace earlier thatching and sometimes slate replaces tile. When a roof looks excessively steep with high crow-steps it is a fair sign that it was covered originally in thatch – either reed, straw or heather.

The medieval harbour has been much rebuilt and strengthened during its long history, often using stone from demolished buildings such as parts of the Castle and perhaps also the Cathedral. The older blocks of masonry, large and roughly squared, are on the northern pier. On the inner pier the more recent harbour works have the stone placed vertically. These upright blocks are held together with iron ties and this form of construction was thought to withstand better the ripping action of currents.

The older fishermen's houses that lined the harbour have mostly disappeared to be replaced by a modern block of flats which looks as if it migrated here from a Mediterranean resort. Not only does this boxy white block spoil the harbourside view but also the setting of the Cathedral ruins and the priory. Old photographs show how attractive this area of cottages once was. Some were even listed buildings, and their demolition shows a poor regard for the town's heritage – a short-sighted decision made by local councillors on our behalf.

To many people, St Andrews is synonymous with golf. Golf brought much wealth and status to St Andrews in the nineteenth century. It was a period of growth for the town; the university expanded, the railways came and the Royal and Ancient Golf Club (the R and A) ruled the golfing world. New hotels were built; big sandstone piles in the Baronial style – Scotland's answer to the Gothic Revival. Some of the hotels catered particularly for golfers, others for holiday-makers. Facing the links, battalions of bays and oriels bedecked in ornate gables and exaggerated crow-steps marched westwards from the R and A.

Golf had probably been played in St Andrews since 1457 when it is said James II forbade the menfolk from playing the game since it interrupted archery practice. Playing the game upset kirk leaders too since it was a common indulgence on Sundays. But the game survived and by 1897, the R and A was the recognised ruling body for the sport. By 1754, the St Andrews Golfers' Club, consisting of 'twenty-two admirers of the ancient and healthful exercise of the Golf', had prepared a list of articles and laws which included amongst others: 'You are not to remove stones, bones or any broken club for the sake of playing your ball. Neither Trench, Ditch or Dyke made for the preservation of the links ... shall be accounted a hazard.'

The Old Course does not belong to the R and A but to the town of St Andrews. The course extends over an area of sand dunes held as common land to the town. In 1552, the rights of warren (to hunt rabbits), held by the archbishop, safeguarded the rights of citizens to play golf. Dating from this time is the quaint

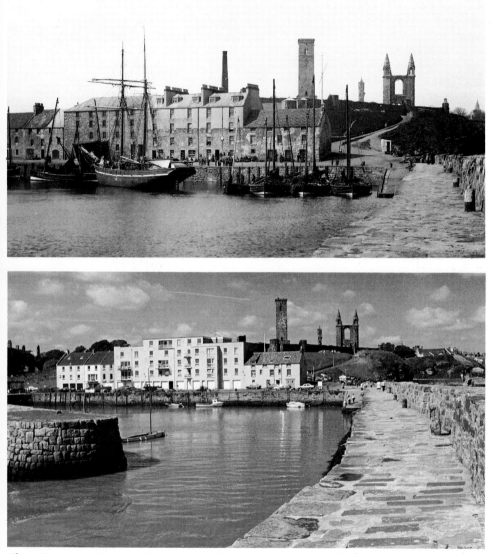

Above: George Washington Wilson's view of St Andrews harbour c. 1880. Below: St Andrews harbour today

old Swilken Bridge which sits picturesquely amongst the greens of the Old Course. Like old teeth, the ancient stones are now held together with iron braces.

The R and A club-house is a building which does not quite live up to its superb positioning or to its name. Neither ancient nor princely, this Victorian building suffers from having been over-extended in its shortish life. Even by the end of the last century, three different architects had been involved in its design. At least recent stone-cleaning has brought to life sandstone detailing long forgotten.

The new hotel built half a mile to the west has become a major landmark – some might say eyesore – on the approach from Cupar. Four storeys high and decidedly rectangular, its boxiness has been reduced of late, by clever use of extensions. Wings have now been added which step the building down from the original box thereby integrating it better into the landscape.

Golf brought prestige to the town and the town responded by building some delightful new streets and terraces. Many of these look rather like scaled-down versions of Edinburgh's late Georgian 'New Town'. Often designed by architects from that city, these additions to the town gave St Andrews a new elegance. They became the houses for the new middle class, who saw the town as a handy commuter area for Dundee.

Many of the Victorian developments were undertaken by James Hope-Scott, who married Sir Walter Scott's granddaughter. Hope-Scott put the family fortune into building speculation, naming the new streets in appropriate fashion. One of the best is Abbotsford Crescent, a long concave crescent of classical houses. On the death of his first wife, he married Lady Victoria Howard and named his final development (Howard Place) after her.

The putting greens which line the links, and the famous golf courses behind, provide a wonderful setting to the town. From the edge of the town the view northwards takes in a marvel-

lous panorama. The golf courses stretching into the distance are edged by silvery sands, beyond them the valley of the Tay and in the distance, on clear days, the hills of Angus. To the right, the North Sea spreads a cold, though often blue, embrace about the town. A few brave Victorian terraces, mostly hotels, face the chill north, their bulk protecting the older parts of town from the elements.

If anywhere in Scotland captures the national mood in architecture and town form, it is surely St Andrews. It is the kind of place whose character depends largely upon the elusive quality of townscape. There are certainly many individual buildings of considerable beauty or interest, but as a town it is the collective character which matters. It is a character whose framework was established by some far-sighted bishops, given substance by a marvellous collection of college buildings, and respected on the whole by countless Georgian and Victorian buildings. Here on a windy plateau above the sea, we have a distinctively Scottish town, a record in stone of the nation's urban tradition.

The Royal and Ancient club-house

Aerial view of Kirkwall

KIRKWALL

Whether you first approach Kirkwall by land or by sea, it is a memorable experience. Attractive groups of old houses huddle together for shelter and protection against the harsh Orkney climate, and above the roof tops rises the splendid red stone Cathedral of St Magnus.

There is little doubt that Kirkwall is one of the best surviving examples of a medieval Norwegian town on either side of the North Sea. The town plan consists of a single long irregular main street with a number of vennels and alleyways running at right angles. The straggling main street is a feature of many Norse towns, such as the street known as Kirkegata in the old town of Stavanger in Norway. Stavanger has much of the urban character of Kirkwall, although the buildings there are made of wood as against Orkney's stone.

There is a sense of mystery and expectation in moving through Kirkwall. The curving main street and the multitude of wynds which lead off it, each inviting exploration, add a healthy measure of complexity to a town which can only be explored on foot. Like a dream where the main characters appear and reappear, often out of context, it takes time to make a reliable mental map of the town.

One cannot exaggerate the importance of climate in shaping the town. Except for the green surrounding the cathedral, no spaces in Kirkwall are large, nowhere is the wind or rain allowed to strike with full force. Microclimates have been created by the town layout, sheltered corners where flowers grow and conversation can be heard above the elements. In most of Britain trees shelter buildings, but on Orkney buildings shelter trees.

The labyrinth of streets and vennels is the perfect urban landscape for Kirkwall's ba' game, the ancient and unique tussle between 'uppies' and 'doonies'. The ba' game has obscure origins, few rules and occurs annually at New Year. It is fought in the streets of the town between two sides of unspecified size: the 'uppies', who seek to transport a leather ball (the ba') to the harbour, and the 'doonies', who score a goal by reaching a wall in the town. It has been likened to a huge loose scrum at rugby football and is played between a team of men from the upper part of town, traditionally under the control of the bishops, and a team from the lower part which was controlled by the earls.

The name Kirkwall comes from the old Norse Kirkjuvagr, which means church by the bay. The crumbling doorway in a close, off Broad Street, is all that remains of the original eleventh-century church of St Olaf. What was once the church, then a poorhouse, is now a residence for the manager of a savings bank.

The Cathedral of St Magnus, which broods over the town of Kirkwall like some ancient oak tree, took over 300 years to build. It was begun in 1137 by Earl Rognvald who chose 'Kirk Bay' as the new capital of Orkney – a capital intended to be the platform for Norse domination of the Hebrides and Isle of Man.

The Norse invaders were a great fighting people and the legends of their heroic acts figure largely in Orkneyinga Saga. It is remarkable that out of such violence comes the beautiful and serene Cathedral of St Magnus – a huge red symbol of peace. Five hundred miles away, the aggressive Normans were similarly responsible in lowland England for some of the finest architecture Britain has ever known. In the north and in the south the invaders brought new ideas, new skills and new blood.

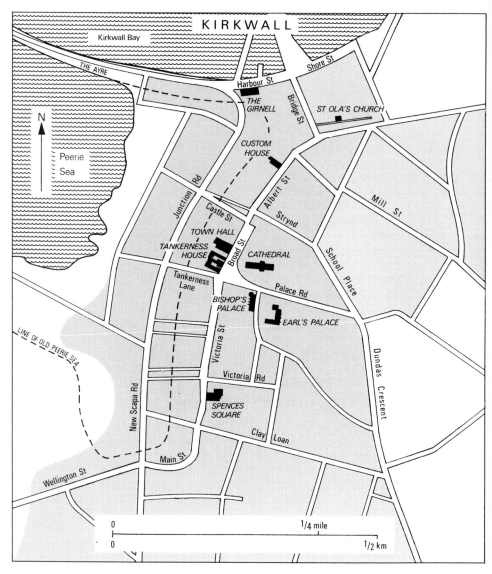

The Norsemen overcame the indigenous Picts, laying waste their brochs and plundering their women. Such barbarism ensured a rich interweaving of bloodstock as modern Kirkwall demonstrates. Not all Norsemen were the blond Viking heroes of legend and the Orkney Earl Thorfinn was described in the sagas thus: 'He was of all men the tallest and strongest; he was ugly; he had black hair, a large nose and a rather dark complexion.'

Before the Norse invaders arrived, Orkney was already a well-populated landscape. Standing stones were commonplace, symbols of spiritual awareness in a scenery of primitive

beauty. The broch builders used simple means to create architecture of pure form, buildings where visual power mattered more than proportion and decoration.

Orkney today is one of those strange marriages of time, where the most ancient and the most modern co-exist in relative harmony. The Ring of Brodgar is a haunting record of man's earliest presence in this remote northern landscape, and at Skara Brae, a village fossilised 5000 years ago by burial in a sudden sandstorm, is preserved a neolithic way of life, a

A wynd in the heart of Kirkwall

35

simple stone technology. Heavily patterned with lichen, the stone shelters served the needs of a self-sufficient community of about thirty people.

There are nine different houses, but in each, the bed to the right of the door is the largest, suggesting it was occupied by the man of the family, who also acted as guard. At Skara Brae, the scarcity of wood meant that builders used only stone and, as stone is imperishable, we have today a perfect picture of Stone Age life on Orkney. Like Pompeii, misfortune in the

Left: Ring of Brodgar

of Orkney; a culture of stark contrasts.

The challenge for the Norsemen was to shape a landscape of rocks, stone and dark gods into a fertile land of farms, small towns and Christian cathedrals. And this is what they achieved. To later generations of Norsemen, we owe the extension of Kirkwall from the bay to the linear form recognisable today. Although the buildings of medieval times have been replaced by stone houses of the seventeenth and eighteenth centuries, many occupy the exact sites of older structures.

Reclamation of land between the straggling main street of Kirkwall and the bay has obscured what was, for centuries, an important relationship. Originally, gardens behind the houses that lined Broad Street and Victoria Street ran down to the Peerie Sea. This was an area of sea sheltered from the main bay by a spit of sand known as The Ayre. The curve of Kirkwall's main street followed the curve of the shore. It is difficult to realise today that just fifty yards away from Broad Street, waves once lapped against the rear walls of the gardens. A view of the town, painted about 1814, shows how close St Magnus once was to the sea. In more recent times, the Peerie Sea has been infilled so that today the town stands some way back from the water's edge.

The town plan is itself like a historic document and reading it gives us a clue to the people who created it. It also tells us of their social organisation. Like other Norse towns, the houses are often arranged gable-end to the long and straggling main street. At its midpoint the street widens to form a market square alongside the Cathedral. This square divides the town into two halves – the upper part being known as Laverock and the lower as Burgh. These two distinct areas still enjoy a degree of rivalry, as witnessed in the ba' game.

Our perception of towns is shaped largely by the routes we elect to take through them. In Kirkwall's case, the most attractive street in

mists of archaeological time has been to our advantage.

Across Scapa Flow on the island of Flotta stands high technology in the form of an oil terminal. Old and new, ancient and modern, megalith and microchip – this is the essence

terms of townscape is also the most used and hence there is a high appreciation of the qualities of the town. These qualities, which make up urban character, have been enhanced by care over the design of paving and shopfronts and by the control of unsuitable development. The centre of Kirkwall is today a conservation area and this is intended to protect and improve the character of the town. Traffic has not been allowed to dominate and consequently spaces are better scaled to the needs of the pedestrian.

There are a few exceptions, however, and these sadly by some best-known household names. Modern shopfronts and shop signs like 'Boots' or 'Woolworths' whch are standardised throughout the United Kingdom make no contribution to the character of old towns. Signs that make no concession to local traditions, are over-sized and dominate the more restrained old shopfronts, should surely be prevented through planning control. But at least

one prominent building society has avoided plastic lettering, perspex fascias and large plate-glass windows, and has entered into the spirit of conservation.

It is not easy to design new buildings which look at home in old settings. Towns are always in a state of change, even if the rate of change is slow as at Kirkwall. New needs have to be met, sometimes by new buildings, sometimes by adapting old. New and old can look happy together as long as a few rules are respected concerning matters such as scale, materials, skyline.

A small housing scheme in Junction Road on part of the reclaimed sea goes some way to resolving the stylistic conflict between old and new. Here the designers have tried to reinterpret the Orcadian tradition of gable-end building, forestairs and small, deeply set windows. Modern space standards and the building regulations prevent the construction of more densely packed houses but the result is still a

climate in the traditional architecture of Scotland. The twentieth century has broken this bond in the cities where tower blocks and windswept acres testify to the futility of fashion at the expense of tradition. But in Kirkwall, and also nearby Stromness, low and densely compacted forms of development have grown up. Public spaces and streets are small, intimate and well protected by surrounding buildings.

Building design responds to climate in much the same way as urban form, and wind and rain are elements to keep out at all costs. The Picts solved the problem by massive windowless walls extending underground with crawl-through entrances. Cracks between masonry were sealed with turf and buildings thrust their thick gables to the wind.

In town house architecture, similar principles can be seen – window sizes are kept to a minimum and set deeply within the walls. Thick flagstone walls often harled on the outside tend to enclose the roofs at gable ends. Eaves barely overhang for fear of their being ripped from the walls by the wind and chimneys are squat and thick helping to hold the roof in a vice-like grip.

reasonable compromise between the Kirkwall tradition and modern utility.

The skill with which a building turns a public corner is a good measure of its success as a design. One of the most important corners in Kirkwall is where Bridge Street joins Harbour Street. At this corner sits the Kirkwall Hotel – a large Victorian building which seems almost to stand guard over the entrance to the historic core of Kirkwall. Facing the harbour, it is an attractive if undistinguished building but turning into Bridge Street it places two large gables high above the narrow street. The effect is to turn the corner with a great deal of assurance and the two gables when viewed down Bridge Street provide a visual stop to the play of traditional gables further up the street. By such means the building's designer has handled the difficult problem of turning a formal front into a rather traditional side elevation more in keeping with the rest of the street.

Town form is closely shaped by function and

Outside Edinburgh and Stirling, few town houses exist from the seventeenth century, yet here there are several. Kirkwall was hardly touched by the improving zeal of the eighteenth century, the industrial zeal of the nineteenth century, or the social zeal of the twentieth century, and so it finds itself today in possession of some of the oldest town houses in Scotland.

By far the best town house is Tankerness House, now Kirkwall's museum, built originally as two manses for cathedral clergymen in the sixteenth century. It is a courtyard house entered from Broad Street, through a heavily moulded archway with armorial panel. It has all the ingredients of Scottish burgh architec-

Far left: Albert Street. Above: the courtyard at Tankerness House ture – crow-steps, turnpike stairs and gabled roofs – yet on a smaller scale than the similar houses in Edinburgh's Lawnmarket. The Latin panel over the doorway reads: 'For country and posterity. Except the Lord watch over it, in vain will our seed have regard for itself.'

In contrast, Kirkwall's later town houses are mostly simple inornate structures of two or three storeys, presenting either a crow-stepped gable or a narrow front to a winding street or close. Houses are normally planned with a room on either side of a central stair with kitchen and washroom behind. Growth tends to be upwards into attic or backwards into the rear garden. Over time, sites soon become heavily built-up, creating the familiar dense texture of the town visible in places like The Strynd.

The Custom House in Albert Street occupies the site of an earlier building which was re-modelled in 1828 by Captain Balfour RN, Provost of Kirkwall. The present building puts a classical frontage onto a building which was once gable-end to the street. It is difficult to design a classical front only two bays wide and here the door is balanced by a window to the left, all set behind a low wall with iron railings. Directly above, the regular pattern of windows continues with a dormer breaking the eaves line and providing a focus at the centre of the composition. Between the upper windows sits the gilded Royal coat of arms. It is a sophisticated design and the use of smooth-painted render sets the building apart from its vernacular neighbours. Inside the house the Georgian detailing continues and the egg-and-dart frieze to the first-floor public rooms and the open-well staircase would do credit to a mansion house on the Scottish mainland.

For traditional street architecture it is difficult to better Victoria Street. Largely free of commercial pressure, the street has hardly changed for a hundred years. Paved in grey-blue Caithness slabs there is barely room for the delivery vans to pass. Dotted along this attractive winding street are a number of in-dividual buildings of great charm and interest. The best is Spences Square, a seventeenth-century group of traditional houses arranged around a small courtyard. Recently converted to flats for the elderly, the architect was careful to preserve the huge stone slates on the roof.

Most Scottish towns are built of stone, and their character varies according to the colour and texture of the local building stone. In Kirkwall, a dark flagstone is the common building stone, often used with pink or orange sandstone for dressings to window and door openings. Each locality has its own distinctive stamp and this is one of the charms of Scottish building. It is therefore sad to see instances where the ancient tradition has been flouted by modern methods of so-called stonework restoration.

In the town, roofs are frequently covered

The Custom House in Albert Street

Stonework detail of head at Spences Square

with Caithness slates. These are thick, often irregularly sized and extremely heavy. They are normally graded so that the large slates occur at the bottom of the roof and the smallest at the top. Copes are normally of stone carved into shallow 'V's and anchored into chimney heads. The use of thin slates, from Easdale or Ballachulish, suggests a more recent building.

As we have noted, lime cement and sea sand is a frequent finish given to stone walls. Harling is a Scottish form of rendering using beach sand, crushed sea shells and lime which is hand-thrown onto the rough stone walls. Not all stonework was harled although sometimes harling has been introduced at a later date, perhaps to cover up subsequent alterations. When the harling is removed today, it often reveals parts of older buildings or arrangements of windows or doors long hidden beneath the cement. An example of this is the old

grocer's shop, 'Stout and Tindall', in Bridge Street. The peeling off of the harling reveals that the stonework was once too dressed to have been originally covered; and also that the present shopfront with its big Victorian windows is an alteration made to a much older building. Unfortunately, harling often covers up a lot of interest and is used more frequently today than former practice would warrant.

When buildings have been demolished in the past, it was common practice to rescue a carved lintel or other detail and incorporate it into the new building. Consequently, a building which bears a date-stone of, say, 1619, may not actually be that old – only the single stone. This is sometimes confusing but it does ensure a sense of continuity in which even the relatively modern county council buildings participate.

In Bridge Street, an older house has been

extended towards the street by building a new front. Only a few feet wide, it shows how scarce building land had become by the 1880s. The new front gives the older house a regular and rather boxy appearance but interestingly, not only is the new work dated (1882) but the date-stone and initials from the former building (1628) have been removed and placed in the extension. It is a clever way of explaining a small piece of local history.

Some carved stones show the tools of the trade of the original occupant, whilst others are decorated with birds and flowers. Generally, the builder or first occupant of the house has his initials and date on a lintel or skew-putt. It is a practice we could usefully revive today; the public display of the authorship and date of the building can only raise design standards and encourage accountability.

Exploring a historic town on foot is rather like reading a good novel. The story unfolds against a complex background and it is only towards the end that the pattern emerges with any clarity. Towns which are predictable and place order above variety can be rather dull places. Historic towns tend to embody richness of experience, a cultural layering where memory is expressed in old buildings and time-trodden streets.

A sense of place requires more than just space between buildings. Place is an elusive quality – there has to be human activity and attractive finishes. Kirkwall's market square, the only major space in the town, is a hotch-potch of ill-fitting parts. This space needs a unifying paving scheme more reminiscent of a public square and the removal of the sad little municipal flower beds.

The Town Hall does not enhance the square; it is a rather large building by Kirkwall standards and almost competes in size with St Magnus which sits opposite. Built in 1884, it replaced the old Tolbooth which had stood

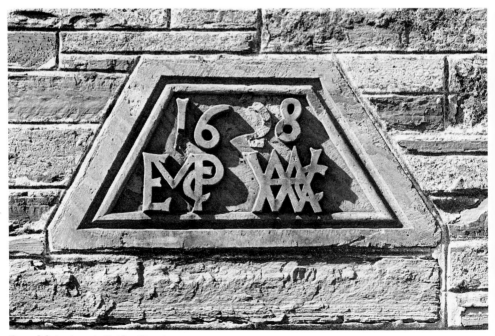

Carved date-stone in Bridge Street

nearby for nearly 300 years. The increase in power and influence of the local authorities in the nineteenth century led to the building of some excellent town halls, often as in Kirkwall at the expense of medieval tolbooths. But this Town Hall in a highly romantic Scottish Baronial style seems to have drawn its inspiration from the castles of the imagination rather than the real thing. It looks out of place amongst the more rugged and solid buildings of the town and only the ancient cathedral can withstand its dominating presence.

St Magnus Cathedral is a magnificent building, part Romanesque, part Gothic, but all united by a wonderful sense of proportion. To a visitor used to the vast Gothic structures of buildings like York Minster, it may seem small, but in the context of Kirkwall and the northern landscapes it is huge.

Looking at St Magnus today, one is struck by the consistency of detailing and the close affinity St Magnus has with Durham Cathedral and Dunfermline Abbey. The plan form – a simple cruciform church with an eight-bay nave, transepts and a three-bay choir – was the model adopted through much of western Europe in the twelfth century. Durham was finished four years before work began at St Magnus. It seems possible, even likely, that the master mason for Romanesque Durham was employed at Kirkwall, perhaps even stopping off to advise at Dunfermline Abbey en route.

The choir and transepts were finished first and would have been in use whilst building work proceeded in the nave. We tend to think of cathedrals as being simply the colour of natural stone but St Magnus was once painted in a formal design of red and black. Some of these decorative designs survive, showing that the interior was once covered in flowing patterns based upon a simple representation of foliage.

Most of the stone for St Magnus Cathedral comes from within five miles of Kirkwall. The

George Washington Wilson's view of St Magnus Cathedral c. 1880

St Magnus interior showing Romanesque details

stone is mostly a mixture of local flagstone layed in clay used as rubble with red sandstone facings. There is an unusual banding of red and white stone in sections of both the external and internal walling – a treatment which anticipates by six centuries the Victorian love of mixing different colours of stone or brick.

Restoration of ancient buildings poses some difficult questions. Should the old stonework, perhaps 800 years old, be repaired at all and if so, can we reliably imitate the original? When the ancient stones are badly eroded, it may be a matter of conjecture to know the precise design the master mason adopted. Conjecture is no basis for restoring an ancient cathedral, yet the old stonework requires some attention, otherwise the building will, in time, simply fall down. If you view an old building as a faithful record of the past, then you should avoid speculative repair. But there are times when enough of the original detailing survives on adjoining stones to give a reliable guide for restoration, and at the south transept doorway of St Magnus, the modern mason has been careful to copy faithfully the original design.

Although St Magnus was, in its early days, part of the ecclesiastical province of Trondheim in Norway, there is nothing distinctly Norse about it. In fact, the reverse is often true, for most of the great churches of Norway were built by British craftsmen, and Trondheim Cathedral in particular is known to have been built with the help of Scottish masons. So the exchanges were two-way when Orkney was under Norse rule.

Building a Gothic cathedral was a bit like making a great ocean liner. There was a co-ordinating designer – usually a senior master mason – beneath whom served various nationalities of skilled craftsmen. At Kirkwall, the designer was from the Durham School and his master plan was built with masons drawn from a wide area, some apparently from France. The carpenters were probably part Norwegian, part English, for the imported oaks were accompanied by skilled craftsmen. The early glass was possibly imported from Germany and so on. Although it took 300 years to build St Magnus, during which time the Orkneys had reverted to Scottish rule (1468), there is a unity about the final building. The sturdy Romanesque arches with their dogtooth mouldings and great fat columns create an interior of power and majesty.

Cathedrals, unlike castles, have a propensity for survival, and Kirkwall, like Glasgow, was fortunate enough to avoid serious damage during the Reformation. The only major change to the Cathedral occurred in the nineteenth century, when a new spire was added after the original was struck by lightning. Sadly, the new spire has a Scandinavian spikiness, which is rather out of keeping with the solid Romanesque character of the remainder.

When we look at St Magnus today we are impressed by the age of the building – 800 years and still going strong. But its age is nothing to the age of the stone from which it is constructed. The stone, an Old Red Sandstone of Orcadian origin, is about 350 million years old. We date buildings by their year of construction but there is an altogether older world in their stones. Geological timescale puts our human endeavours into perspective.

Another building of great interest in Kirkwall is the Earl's Palace. It has been described as not only the finest secular building in Orkney, but also one of the most mature and accomplished pieces of Renaissance architecture in Scotland. The palace had one of the most impressive staterooms of any private castle in Scotland. Here Earl Patrick would entertain in a magnificent room of large bow windows, tapestries and what must have been one of the widest fireplaces in Britain. The size of a fireplace was a good measure of the social standing of a man in the seventeenth century. This one with its elaborately carved jambs, and span of fifteen feet, was so impressive that alongside it Sir Walter Scott set the meeting of Clement Cleveland and Frederick Altmont in his novel *The Pirate*.

Few masons trusted a single arch to carry a great weight, so there is also a relieving arch above the fireplace to share in the job of supporting the weight of the chimney. Notice how the voussoirs or arch stones are joggle-jointed or kinked to prevent them slipping. Again, we find the stonework of recent restoration clearly left to look new and not disguised as old. But the palace is partly ruined and sadly roofless and for its qualities to come alive, you need both a trained eye and a fair amount of imagination.

George Washington Wilson, the great Victorian recorder of Scottish monuments through the new medium of photography and, incidentally, photographer royal to Queen Victoria, captured a view of the Palace's great hall before its fossilisation at the hands of the Ancient Monuments Board. Today, the vegetation has gone and also much of the romance and in their place we have a great deal of pointing and sad little signs. Tourism is big business in Scotland but tourists do seem to be treated in a dull and unimaginative fashion.

The same can be said about the less interesting although older Bishop's Palace, built in the mid-twelfth century for Bishop William the Old, friend of Earl Rognvald. Built right next to the Cathedral, it consisted of a hall used for festive occasions and a tower house from which the bishop kept an eye on his growing St Magnus. The Bishop's Palace originally conformed to the plan of a royal Norwegian palace, with a great long hall above cellars.

The use of relieving arches is commonplace in Scotland's historic buildings. The lintel was hardly ever trusted on its own to carry the weight of what could be tens of tons of masonry. Instead, the lintel was used with one or two arches set in the stonework above. It was a kind of belts-and-braces way of holding up your trousers. In the Bishop's Palace, the hall has a fireplace set in the south wall which has a lintel and two relieving arches to support the overhead stonework, but even this was not enough for the lintel is cracked.

The Earl's Palace built in 1600

The Bishop's Palace

Infilling of adjoining open space is a common way of expanding buildings in Kirkwall. Land soon becomes eaten up as new buildings are constructed often directly alongside old. Buildings gable to gable, with barely a couple of feet between them, are commonplace. Tiny windows look into gloomy passages providing ventilation, just a little light but a lot of shelter. Sometimes these narrow slots between buildings are actually filled, although not all as elegantly as at 20 Harbour Street. Here the doorway has an attractive Georgian fanlight and is surrounded by an arch of red and white voussoirs which seems to imitate the much older practice at St Magnus.

Nearby in Harbour Street stands the Girnell which was once the store for oats and meal paid as rent by tenants of the Earl. The word Girnell means chest and the forestairs on the outside gave access from the nearby corn slip at the harbour to the storage rooms above. The stonework gives away the fact that once there were two forestairs facing the harbour but one has subsequently been removed – perhaps when Thomas Telford rebuilt the harbour in 1809.

Although Kirkwall has maintained its medieval street character and kept most of its early Norse buildings, there have been some losses in recent years, which have eroded the integrity of the historic town. With old towns, the supporting role of lesser buildings is always important and you remove them at your peril. Shore Street has borne the brunt of demolition and attractive rows of gable-end houses have disappeared to make way for an oil depot, car parks and road widening. Whatever the added convenience, areas of asphalt are no substitute for historic character. Each age has added something of value to Kirkwall but ours promises to leave a legacy of clearance and widening in a town whose urban character stems from being close-grained, sheltered and compact.

Aerial view of Crail

CRAIL

Until the Industrial Revolution, most of the people of Scotland lived near the sea, either on the mainland or in countless scattered communities around the islands. The sea provided obvious advantages: an abundant source of food, a means of transport, and along the shore and cliffs, a supply of building materials for constructing harbours and houses. All that was needed was a sheltered cove, a good supply of fresh water and an area of coastal land for crops and animals. This was the pattern for countless early communities, all surviving on a healthy diet consisting largely of herring, crabs, oysters, oats and kale.

As the small towns prospered some were given special trading rights under Royal Charters. Crail was one such town; it became a Royal Burgh in 1178. As such, it is one of the oldest Royal Burghs in Scotland and was, for a time, one of the wealthiest. Today, it is the least spoilt of all the Royal Burgh seaside towns, having survived the industrialisation and urban change of the nineteenth century by good fortune and through geographical isolation. Crail remains the most picturesque of several ancient harbour towns, known as the East Neuk towns, which extend around the Fife coast between Culross in the west and St Andrews in the east.

Crabs, lobsters and smoked fish have always been the mainstay of Crail's economy and the remains of an old haddock-smoking factory for producing Crail Capons exist at the back of the beach. But Crail's wealth in earlier centuries was the result of commerce and trade as much as fishing. As one of the trading centres between Scotland and the Low Countries, the old port brought much prosperity to the town. This wealth is reflected today, not just in its surviving houses and public buildings, but in the way Crail's town plan has been generated with trade very much in mind.

The plan of Crail contains three separate market squares – Marketgate, Nethergate and High Street. The use of the word 'gate' derives from the Norse 'gata' meaning street, rather than gateway in Anglo-Saxon. Of these, the Nethergate is the oldest, consisting of a widened stretch of street for outdoor markets, typical of Scottish towns of the medieval period. Nethergate was an impressively large market square by the standards of the Middle Ages although subsequent infilling of the open space has reduced its impact today.

The part of Crail immediately north of the harbour and around the long demolished castle is the most ancient. It has an irregularity of street layout, a smallness of scale and atmosphere of centuries of use which few Scottish towns possess. The area has much the atmosphere of walking through an ancient cathedral. Here many of the older houses have forestairs, evidence that it was used by a craftsman – weaver, leatherworker, sailmaker – with the craft being undertaken beneath the stair.

In this, the oldest quarter of Crail, the streets and wynds are narrow, curving left and right, apparently without plan, gardens are tiny or non-existent and buildings are huddled together as a protection against the harsh seaside climate. Stone, often quarried from the sea cliffs nearby, is the principal building material. It is used to make walls, roads, steps, paving and the harbour itself. Even the bollards along the harbour walls are made of stone rather than iron.

Timber was widely used in earlier centuries but by 1600 had become scarce and expensive

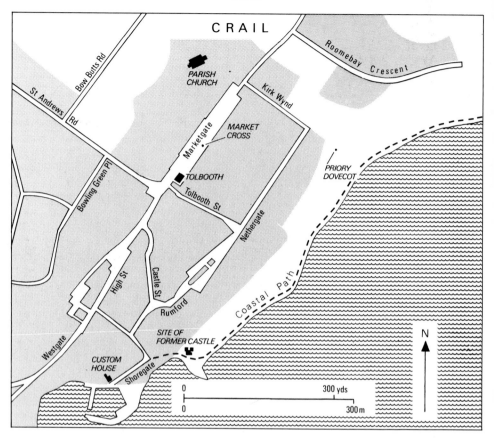

and its use was restricted to floors, roofs and boat-building. Roofs are generally covered in clay pantiles, although they would originally have been thatched. Pantiles were imported into Scotland from Holland as ballast and return cargoes in the boats which had exported Scottish woollens, mutton and salted herrings. Roofs covered in slate tend to be of more recent origin, although older pantiled roofs often have lower courses of slate to prevent entry by birds into the roof space via the folds of the pantiles. The skirting of pantiled roofs by slate is a common feature of Fife towns.

In the past, it was often common practice for the tar and paint used to protect the boats to be applied to buildings, either as a wall coating or as a protection to windows and doors. Consequently, boats and buildings tended to have the same colour treatment, ensuring a colourful patchwork around the harbour areas. Today, the distinction between marine paint and masonry paint has broken this endearing tradition and whites and greys now tend to replace, for walls at least, the brighter colours seen in the past.

Around the harbour and up to the High Street, walls are often harled. Harling, used with and without stone dressings, gives older buildings an appearance of rough solidity which modern building construction lacks. Added to this, windows are small, roofs are steep and ended with crow-steps – a form of

The roofscape of Crail

building design which is in response rather than opposition to climate. The tradition becomes almost a style which not only unites the various structures of Crail but gives all of the East Neuk towns a certain similarity.

Crow-stepped gables are a common feature of old Scottish houses. They are the result of the difficulty of cutting sandstone on a diagonal. Being a sedimentary rock, sandstone splits along its bed and hence square blocks result. These square blocks are built on top of the gable wall with the roof butting against it. It is the natural way to finish a wall with sandstone, for tradition generally follows economy of means, and has the added advantage of providing steps from which to inspect and mend the roof.

Generally speaking, the wealthy houses present their long fronts to the street, the poor houses only their gables. The contrasting pattern of eaves and gables, of stone and harl, of tile and slate, of tall and low, all combine to make up the characteristic townscape of late medieval Scotland. Here in Crail, the effect is further enhanced by the curving streets, spacious market squares and glimpses of the sea between close-packed buildings.

Form, function and climate are closely interrelated in these coastal communities. There is little one would call style in the modern sense – the individual buildings and the town itself are the result of using and re-using well-tried methods, plus typical Scottish thrift and resourcefulness. Craftsmanship plays a large part, where the skills of the hand and the trained eye turn the mundane into an object of pleasure. But craftsmanship was not just the preserve of architecture; the old boats in the harbour also share the same common language.

King Street at the approach to the harbourside

The upper part of Crail shows signs of having been consciously planned. With the growing prosperity which followed the awarding of the Royal Charter in the twelfth century, the burgesses made deliberate decisions regarding the expansion of the early harbour town. Two roughly parallel streets – High Street and Marketgate – were created in the early sixteenth century following the angle of the shore, but set further inland than the old market street.

The expanded town was enclosed by an enlarged town wall which surrounded the whole town of Crail.

In 1503, it was by Act of Parliament, 'statute and ordanit that all tounis and portis on the sey side, sik as Leth, Inverkethin, Kingorne, Disert, Crail and otheris, war spend their commone gudis one the wallis of thair toune to the sey side with portis of lyme and stane.'

The wall was as much for keeping animals out of the town as a protection against the supposed English invaders, for the open Scottish landscapes were not yet enclosed and animals wandered at will. The town wall also controlled the movement of goods for which local taxes had to be paid – taxes which paid for the upkeep of the town. Sadly, little of the original town wall at Crail survives today, although later walls are very much part of its character.

The two new streets of the fifteenth and sixteenth centuries were the result more of deliberate decisions by the burgesses, than of strict formal planning in the modern sense. These streets were not laid out in geometric fashion – this came two or three centuries later to Scotland – instead they represented a more relaxed form of planning which respected existing features like rocks or hills, working around rather than obliterating them. It was really the sort of plan one would make for a garden, responding to the site rather than imposing one's will regardless. The planning at Crail is remarkably like a small version of St Andrews, with two roughly parallel streets lined by houses with long thin gardens behind called 'rigs' or burgess strips.

The pattern of development in medieval Scotland was based upon a unit of property known as the 'rig'. This was the standard parcel of land ownership for many of the wealthy traders or craftsmen. In Crail, it consisted normally of a narrow-fronted plot to the main street or market square, the garden running back for some distance, perhaps to the town wall. As a result land ownership consisted of long fingers of land, some only a few metres wide, running parallel to each other somewhat like the pattern of medieval strip farming.

The burgesses or traders built their houses on the street front, generally filling the whole frontage. Access to the rear gardens and adjoining countryside was via arched pends or alleyways. Wealthy traders had wide-fronted plots, poorer artisans had narrow plots, producing the familiar play of full-fronted and gable-end houses in carefree juxtaposition along the street. Outside stairs and crow-stepping added further interest to the scene.

As a trading town, markets were especially important to Crail and until the nineteenth century, when the first shops began to appear, all trading was carried out in the open air or within the rudimentary shelter of a market stall. The crab stalls of today are part of this centuries-old tradition.

Whether you approach Crail by land or sea, the two spires of Kirk and Tolbooth break the skyline. Positioned at the top of the town, these two vertical symbols of ecclesiastical and secular power herald your arrival. Like all the fishing towns of the East Neuk, each settlement marks its presence by a variety of towers and spires. On a grey day in the North Sea, it is important that each town can be immediately recognised from the water. In the open Fife landscapes, the spire has a special function, as a guide to the traveller and, once you have learnt to read the language of the different combinations of spires, as a means of identifying each town. Crail is relatively simple: two spires; one tall, the other more square and shaped. St Andrews had three spires and a tower, Anstruther two spires and a tower. The pattern of spires, changing at each burgh, established a kind of simple graphic code for fishermen, mariners and pilgrims alike. In a sense, each town had a signature on the landscape all of its own.

Kirk and Tolbooth were essential to the functioning of a Royal Burgh. Both were key public buildings and as such enjoyed special positioning in the town. The church at Crail is set apart from the bustle of the town in a quiet churchyard. The seclusion invites meditation within the safe confines of the medieval wall. The Tolbooth, on the other hand, stands at a road crossing, where Marketgate leads into High Street and hence via Castle Street down to the harbour. Its position symbolises the importance of commerce in the life of Crail.

Friar Court in Marketgate built in 1686

The first reference to a church at Crail occurs in the middle of the twelfth century, but the present church of St Mary was consecrated 100 years later. Little of the early church survives except the tower where, at its base, deep grooves show that medieval archers once used the stones to sharpen their steel-tipped arrows. It is said that townsmen fighting for King Robert the Bruce sharpened their arrows here for divine guidance but it is more likely that later bowmen used the open churchyard for archery practice. In any event, we should be grateful that the Victorian restorers left this feature for our enjoyment.

St Mary's became a Collegiate Church in the sixteenth century when the local laird, Sir William Myrton, made a rich endowment in return for daily prayers being said on his behalf. It was a means, popular at the time, whereby wealthy landowners tried to buy their way to heaven. Myrton also established a grammar school and a school of music but

after the Reformation in 1587, James VI granted the church with its endowments to the bailies of the burgh.

Evidence of much earlier religious activity exists in a number of carved slabs and monuments. Against the inner face of the church wall at the west entrance is a finely sculptured slab bearing a cross of Celtic design decorated with key pattern and interlaced work. Barely discernible are a number of carvings in the relief of animals and birds helping to date the slab to about the ninth century. There are several monuments and tombstones of interest in the churchyard but my favourite is the square battlemented deadhouse with the chilling inscription: 'Erected for securing the dead.' It was built in 1826, the age of Burke and Hare and other body-snatchers.

The Tolbooth is the other public building of interest and incorporates in its fabric decayed fragments of the demolished Kirk of the twelfth century. The lower portion of the Tolbooth

Below: Crail church. Right: detail of grooves formed by sharpening steel-tipped arrows

tower dates from before 1517 and contains, set in the rubble walling on its south side, a much earlier capital and base which once decorated the Kirk. The Tolbooth performed many functions; it was a prison and a retreat for the burgesses in times of trouble. It was also the building where taxes were collected, and the law administered. From the Tolbooth, the burgesses exercised their power, and this building, like that at Musselburgh across the Forth, has all the marks of civic pride.

The Tolbooth tower at Crail, whose upper part dates from around 1600, shows strong Dutch influence in its design. It was not so much that Dutch designers were used but that the Scottish traders picked up fashions and ideas from across the North Sea and applied them at home. Trade was not only an exchange of goods and commodities, it involved an exchange of culture and of values. It is hard to visualise Crail today as being at the sharp end of art and design but for much of medieval Scotland, east-coast ports like Crail were the entry points for new ideas, new fashions and new architecture.

The Tolbooth spire is crowned with a weathercock in the form of a gilded 'Crail Capon' – a haddock dried in the sun or smoked in the fire. Inside hangs a bell probably from an earlier Tolbooth which bears the inscription in Dutch: 'I was cast in the year of our Lord 1520.' By ancient custom, it was rung at 10 pm each night as a warning for decent burgesses to head for their beds. In the eastern extension to the Tolbooth there is inserted a panel bearing the coat of arms of the burgh as represented on the common seal. It shows a single-masted ship, a crescent moon and six stars. The top of the panel bears the date 1602 with the name Crail below.

There was a strict hierarchy in burgh affairs. The burgesses, with their strips of property secured originally from the Crown, controlled local government. It was usually the merchant burgesses who managed the affairs of the Royal Burghs to the exclusion of the crafts-

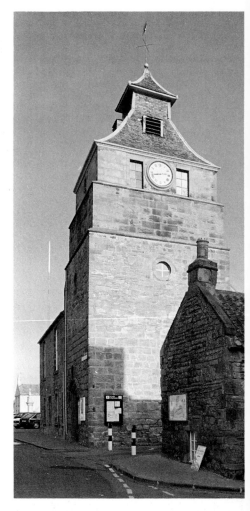

men. However, in 1583 James VI decreed that craftsmen should have formal representation on Town Councils but much antagonism remained between the Merchant Guilds and the Craft Guilds. With the merchants enjoying trading monopolies into the seventeenth century on even staple commodities their social position remained largely unchanged.

No medieval town in Scotland was complete without a market cross. It marked the point where trade was officially carried out and public pronouncements made. Most surviving market crosses are of post-Reformation date and the cross at Crail is no exception – a relatively modern King's unicorn above a seventeenth-century stone shaft. But its symbolic value to the commercial life of the burgh was more important than the age of the stone. Until 150 years ago, when the first shops began to appear, the market cross was in a sense the supermarket check-out of olden days, the point where the money flowed.

Like all historic towns, the history of the place is written in the stones, and in the town plan, rather than in historic manuscripts. There are few written records of Crail as old as the structures themselves and few structures as old as the town plan. In towns like Crail with perhaps 1000 years of continuous occupation, few buildings endure as long as the street layout. In this period, Crail has lost practically all traces of its royal castle, nunnery and priory. Discovering remnants of these today is a matter more for archaeology but they have left their mark in Crail in terms of street names and, of course, town layout.

Being able to read the clues in the buildings is part of the enjoyment of old towns. As we go back in time, we are forced to depend more upon ancient structures and man's imprint upon the landscape for clues to our history.

The harbour at Crail is no exception. There are only scant records of the building of the harbour walls, yet by 1583, reference is made to the existence of a decent harbour. Subsequent rebuilding has blurred the differentiation between medieval and later construction. The extension to the west pier is known to be the work of the engineer Robert Stevenson and dates from 1828. Stevenson had the idea of building a wooden boom to close off the harbour entrance during rough weather and this structure still survives. Whenever it was built the fortress-like harbour sends its curving walls out like ramparts into the North Sea.

Before the present harbour was built, boats were probably just drawn up the sandy beach. It must have been a busy beach, however, for in the thirteenth century Crail is reputed to have supplied the royal household with rabbits from the Isle of May.

Left: Crail Tolbooth. Below: George Washington Wilson's view of Crail harbour c. 1880

The Priory Dovecot: interior showing nesting boxes

Viewing the harbour 100 years ago, one gets a good idea of the bustle of activity which must have characterised Crail in past times. One of the pioneers of Scottish landscape photography, George Washington Wilson, provides us with memorable views of the harbour in the 1880s. Regretfully, the sundial which stood for 200 years by the harbour was moved in 1883 to a new position on the castle promenade. Before we all had wrist-watches and wall clocks, sundials performed a valuable function, especially when tides had to be carefully watched. The sundial was once part of the working landscape of the harbour, now it is a mere seaside decoration. Along the coastal path to the east, another functional survivor from the past – although thankfully in its original position – is the priory dovecot. It is a cylindrical dovecot with high-level drum entry and shows again the importance of the dove to the life of the monasteries.

The pattern of rigs survives well at Crail. Ownership of a rig was a considerable privilege and sign of social status. Each burgess had to enclose his rig with a high stone wall and to demonstrate who owned the wall a small recess was built into it on the owners' side. These garden walls remain vital elements in the character of the town.

It is relatively easy today to identify where the prosperous merchants lived. Their houses are much grander than the fishermen's cottages and present wide and handsome frontages to the street. From the upper windows the merchants could watch their ships being loaded in the harbour below.

One of the best surviving houses is the Custom House in Shoregate which dates from the seventeenth century. It originally served the semi-official function of keeping the customs and excise records and this is delightfully illustrated in the ship carved into the painted door lintel. The building is taller and deeper than most, signifying its importance. The skew-putts – the lowest crow-step – are carved with initials, anchor and crossed palm leaves. In-side, some of the original panelling survives, giving the rooms the air of being inside a captain's cabin.

Another building with an interesting interior is at 19 Shoregate. This house was extended in the eighteenth century towards the street, burying an old carved lintel behind plaster. Rediscovered recently, the lintel bears the inscription 'John Ottir and Jane Abey – 1613'. The name Ottir is surely of Dutch origin and the moulded door-surround is a fair measure of the man's importance. A tiny staircase window has a check carved into the stone to take the leaded glazing. Ottir probably took the precious glass with him when he was away on business.

Lintels with carved initials and date are called 'marriage lintels', but they are just as likely to represent the initials of the builders of the house and its date as to celebrate a wedding. Often the craft of the occupant is represented in the carving of a lintel or panel. In the wall opposite 12 Castle Street, a cooper's knife and compasses are carved alongside the initials I A I P and date 1643 and another panel, now incorporated into a park bridge in Victoria Gardens, has a carved representation of joiner's tools. Other stones have religious overtones such as 'God's Blessing is my Land and Rent' in Tolbooth Wynd and 'The Lord is my Helper' carved into a panel at 16 High Street.

A building which confronts most visitors arriving by road to Crail is the black and white Golf Hotel in the High Street. In the eighteenth century it was the local coaching inn and still retains a great deal of character associated with the coaching days. Painted in robust traditional fashion and never heavily restored, it is one of the more interesting buildings in Crail. The slightly corbelled-out corner suggests a late medieval tower house as do the many crow-stepped gable attics, some with scrolled skew-putts. On entering the inn, you pass down three steps, a fair sign of antiquity as our roads are reckoned to rise three or four inches every 100 years.

The Golf Hotel was the home of the Crail Golf Society which met here regularly from 1786. In that year 'several Gentlemen ... who were fond of the diversion' founded the Crail Golfing Society, one of the oldest in Scotland. Of the eleven original members one, Daniel Conolly, was proprietor of the inn – hence the name Golf Hotel.

Sadly, the Golf Hotel is now disfigured by a collection of road direction signs and a truly monstrous metal lamp standard. The bullying of an old building by traffic signs and the destruction of its setting by poorly designed street lights is something no building 300 years old deserves.

Too often road and footpath surfaces in Crail do little justice to the quality of design and craftsmanship found in the surrounding buildings. Design should really extend over all the surfaces, not just the façades of buildings, but for some reason the horizontal surfaces that make up the street are just a patchwork of asphalt and concrete. Presentation is important to historic towns and special care needs to be taken over the design of roads and the supporting paraphernalia of signs and lights.

Above: Crail harbour dominated by the three-storey Custom House. Left: detail of ship carved into the stone lintel at Custom House. Right: the Golf Hotel with Tolbooth behind

65

Near the Golf Hotel, at 9 Marketgate, stands a house known as Friar's Court. It is a rather grand house dated 1686, built for a wealthy burgess, although its origins may be older. Built of rubble sandstone with a moulded doorway and crow-steps, the house is typical of the standard of town building demanded by burgesses who were as much at home in Amsterdam as in Edinburgh.

Amongst the wealth of late medieval burgh architecture stands a cool and sophisticated Georgian house. It is called Kirkmay House and dates from 1817. Rather amusingly, it bears an inset lintel in the rear wall positioned upside down with the date 1619 – perhaps rescued from an earlier house on the site. It was perverse to build the lintel the wrong way up and could just be intended to prevent future historians from wrongly dating the building, although the style is so obviously of the Georgian period, that seems hardly likely. As a double-bow-fronted mansion house complete with fly-over stairs and ashlar stonework (smooth polished blocks), it would grace even the best streets of Edinburgh's New Town. Unfortunately, a Victorian attic undermines the elegant proportions.

The Victorians are much maligned for their destruction of cities, yet in Crail their contribution to urban townscape is, on the whole, successful. A good example is a row of five houses in Castle Terrace right in the heart of historic Crail. Each house uses the well-tried language of the Scottish vernacular, yet each is subtly different and at the end of the terrace, overlooking the harbour, a splendid oriel window juts out as proud as the bow of a ship.

It is the richness of the details that counts in historic towns. Small things like foot scrapes and chimney pots add up to make something greater than the sum of the individual parts. At the local pottery, a new detail has been added, quite in character: a ceramic pot for a chimney can. A witty reference to a craft perhaps, but the scale and materials are right, so there is no loss of character.

There are more ways to destroy a historic building than by simply knocking it down. The present fad for door and window replacements, often in aluminium, poses a threat to the character of many old towns. Front doors are crucial since they gesture towards the public

a sort in the Bronze Age and it is likely that some of the coastal caves were occupied by early man. Legend holds that the Scots King Constantine II sought refuge in the nearby caves of Fife Ness in the tenth century, adding his marks to the early Christian crosses scratched into the cave walls.

What place does Crail hold in modern Scotland? It has, of course, known wealthier times, even periods of influence, and the memories of these survive in the many buildings which have come down to us from these distant days. By Scottish standards, Crail provides an unusually long example of continuity – a continuity not just of occupation but of collective endeavour. There is not the sense of boom and bust that you find in many old towns. Instead, each age has added a little to the character of the place without taking much away.

The Scottish people, more than most in Europe, have been much uprooted. Their history is one of settlement and resettlement, of invasion and colonisation. In more recent times, most Scots have had to adjust from a simple rural life to the turmoil of big cities. In the past two or three generations, many have moved from inner slums to life in the new towns. Crail represents an example of urban continuity, of a sense of history and tradition made alive in architecture and planning.

domain. Too often a slick aluminium door of standardised design replaces an old door of character and historic interest, as in a building at the east end of Marketgate.

Crail's history extends further back than records exist. There is evidence of a settlement of

A row of Victorian houses in Castle Terrace

Aerial view of Kirkcudbright. Overleaf: old cottages on the banks of Moat Brae

KIRKCUDBRIGHT

Compared to most Scottish towns, Kirkcudbright is a colourful place. Rows of attractive Georgian houses have been painted in combinations of reds, blues and blacks, producing an effect which is almost continental, and certainly not Scottish. It was the famous Victorian art critic, John Ruskin, who once said you could judge the mental health of a nation by its use of colour. He wrote, 'You will find ... your power of colouring depends much on your state of health and right balance of mind; colour power is a great sign of mental health in nations; when they are in a state of intellectual decline, their colouring always gets dull.' On these grounds modern Kirkcudbright is a healthy place but there is more to the town than a splash of colour.

Kirkcudbright, like the other seaside towns featured in the series, is an ancient place. There has been continuous occupation of this area of marshy ground by the Dee estuary since the eighth century when it was colonised by the Vikings. They established the Christian Church of St Cuthbert's near the town. It survives today only in the place name Kirk-Cuthbert, and a few fragmentary remains just east of the town. A gruesome reminder of these early days survives in the town seal which shows St Cuthbert with the head of the martyred St Oswald, King of Northumbria, in his lap.

The Vikings helped spread Christianity to this part of Scotland, cementing the new religious belief with an iron fist and a programme of church building. But the old beliefs died hard and for a time both pagan and Christian traditions existed side by side or were fused into a single ceremony. There is a legend that in 1165, Ailred of Rievaulx visited Kirkcudbright on the feast day of St Cuthbert and discovered to his horror that bull-baiting was being carried out as part of the Christian festival. Ailred tried to intervene but was rebuked by the young men, who told him to mind his own business. However, the bull exercised 'divine retribution' by goring one of the baiters.

By the twelfth century, Kirkcudbright had become established as the centre of regional government, exercised by Fergus, Lord of Galloway, whose motte-and-bailey castle is supposed to lie just outside of town. The growing importance of the town in these early days is well demonstrated by Edward I's visit to Kirkcudbright for ten days in 1300. He probably stayed at Castledykes, a courtyard castle, whose earthwork remains can be traced today in the meadows just west of the town. Castledykes was once fully comparable in size and design with Caerlaverock Castle along the Dumfriesshire coast. It was a rectangular castle with four round corner towers and drawbridge entrance over a water-filled ditch.

Kirkcudbright has had a violent past. For a long time two nations faced each other across the Solway in a state of open hostility. The resulting concern for defence from without, as well as the need for safety within, led to much castle and dyke building. Kirkcudbright's defences consisted of a water-filled ditch and wall to enclose the town on the west and south sides, known as the Fosse, a natural creek to the east and the River Dee to the north. The general marshy state of the surrounding land added much to the town's natural defences. There were two gates into the town, one at the old harbour side and the other known as Meikle Yett at the entrance to High Street.

Lengths of the Fosse survive, but the Meikle

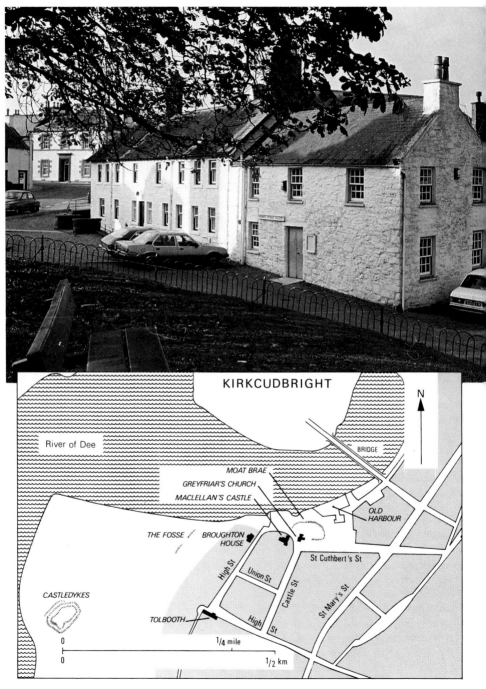

the Old Greyfriar's Church and Meikle Gate at either end and the Tolbooth at the angle or hinge. The result was a long street with a single name bending abruptly through a right angle. Building plots were generally narrow and rear gardens extended backwards for some length, often as far as the estuary or defensive wall. This 'rig' pattern of land ownership is typical of burgh planning of the medieval period, and we have already encountered it in Crail and St Andrews.

The 'rig' system produces the characteristic townscape of gable-end houses to the street mixed with the wider-fronted houses of the richer merchants. Access to rear gardens or common grazing land was through arched closes or pends opening from the main street. Later, expansion was accommodated by buildings being added to the rear, often in stepped fashion. It made for picturesque compositions as in the old houses near the Tolbooth, which in time were fully exploited by artists.

This pattern of urban development, which is essentially Scottish rather than English or European in character, had a clearly defined sense of territory and privacy. The street was a public area open to all and sundry, the close or wynd was semi-public shared by a handful of families, the rear gardens were semi-private used by one or two families but overlooked by neighbours, and the houses themselves were private – a world apart. The boundaries between these different territories were defined by gateways, doorways and changes in paving design. The hierarchy of privacy was clearly expressed in architecture and layout.

Yett – rebuilt in 1590, so that the contractor, Herbert Gledstunes, when riding his horse, 'may not reik the hand to the pier stane thereof' – was removed in 1771 after a deputation had claimed, 'the gate, called the Meikle Yett, while it forms a separation of one part of the town from the other part, gives not advantages to the one part and is hurtful to the rest'. Its demolition marked the end of a period where defence had been a major factor in shaping the town and the beginning of a new age of expansion under the influence of settled times and new enlightened values.

Before we look at the planned expansion of Kirkcudbright in the eighteenth century, it is necessary to understand the growth of the town in the preceding centuries. Within the confines of the defensive ditches, the town developed to form an 'L'-shaped High Street with

In Kirkcudbright, most of the public buildings of the late medieval period have survived but few of the original merchants' houses exist, although their foundations may well lie beneath the walls of existing structures. The notable survivors of the fifteenth and sixteenth centuries are the Tolbooth, Maclellan's Castle and parts of Greyfriar's Church, although this has really been modernised to the point where it has been stripped of much of its interest.

A narrow lane leading off High Street

Maclellan's Castle

The Victorian restorers were often vandals in disguise, transforming old buildings rich in interest and antiquity to a unified and tidy replica of the original. This is the sad fate that befell the fifteenth-century Franciscan Priory Church of Greyfriars, first in 1838 when it was converted to a school and then early in the present century, when it was reconverted to a church. Only the aisle of the old church survives. Near the church lies Moat Brae which is all that remains of a twelfth-century motte which was part of a Fergus, Lord of Galloway, castle. From here and other castles on Deeside, Fergus ran a considerable provincial empire before he retired to Holyrood Abbey in Edinburgh to become an Augustinian abbot.

Nearby Moat Brae and still dominating the town, stands the great hulk of Maclellan's Castle. It was once a sixteenth-century fortified tower house-cum-town mansion for Sir Thomas Maclellan, who had the good fortune to benefit from the dissolution of the monasteries. In 1569 he acquired the lands and buildings of the Greyfriar's Convent and dismantled most of the buildings to provide stone for his new castle.

Maclellan's Castle is not really a castle, more a spacious town house with defensive overtones. The building represents a transition between the genuine Scottish border castle of the fifteenth century and the early classical mansions of the seventeenth. Hence there are elements which look both backwards and forwards in design terms – gun-loops from the past and spacious, well-proportioned halls of the future.

The size and splendour of the castle is unusual for the period and reflects Maclellan's grandiose vision and the exceptional wealth he enjoyed at the church's expense. But the building of the castle and the maintenance of a private army was to prove the family's downfall and in 1664, most of the estate was sold to creditors. By 1752, the roof was stripped by its new owner, Sir Robert Maxwell, who was anxious to re-use the timbers. In 1782, the ruin and other town land was sold to the Earl of Selkirk, a man who left his mark for the good of the town.

Maclellan's Castle is the type of building which inspired the national romantic movement of the nineteenth century – commonly called the Scottish Baronial style. The abstract, almost cubic qualities of massing, the large areas of wall with windows punched through, the tall chimney stacks and corner turrets, were all features reinterpreted and exploited by Scottish architects of the late Victorian period.

The Glasgow architect Charles Rennie Mackintosh, in a lecture given in 1891, said of the castles of the period: 'In the castles of the fifteenth century, every feature was useful. In the sixteenth century also, however exaggerated some of the corbels and other features might be, they are still distinguished from the later examples of the seventeenth century by their genuineness and utility. Since then, we have had no such thing as a national style, sometimes we have been Greek, sometimes Italian and again Gothic ... It was ... the architecture of our own country, just as much Scotch as we are ourselves – as indigenous to our country as our wild flowers, our family names, our customs or our political constitution.' Mackintosh made this built heritage a living tradition. The national style was reborn only to be lost a generation later in the tidal wave of international modernism.

The entrance to Maclellan's Castle is set in the angle between the two wings. Most Scottish castles are so arranged to provide a high level of surveillance over those seeking entry. Normally gun-loops overlook this area, but comfort rather than security was now the overriding concern. Comfort was just what Sir Thomas Maclellan sought in his castle. A spacious stair leads to the first floor where the main living quarters are to be found, including the splendid great hall.

Here in the great hall, Maclellan, as Provost of Kirkcudbright, could entertain his guests in style. No doubt they discussed the shifting of power from the rule of the church to the rule of the state as they warmed themselves by the enormous fireplace, burning timbers perhaps from the broken-up monasteries. Over ten feet wide and supported by a single granite lintel and two relieving arches, the fireplace would have had a fire burning continuously through the winter months. The fireplace has an intriguing spy-hole (Laird's Lug) in the back for watching over the great hall and eavesdropping on the conversation from a private room reached from the stair. Many a useful secret must have come Maclellan's way through this spy-hole. As Provost, he needed to know what was being said behind his back, as much as to his face.

From the large rectangular windows, Provost Maclellan could look down the High Street to the Market Square and in the opposite direc-tion across the harbour to the Dee Estuary. His view was of small trading ships and merchants going about their business. In 1655, Thomas Tucker, a Cromwellian government official, described Kirkcudbright as: 'a pretty place and one of the best ports on this side of Scotland ...'

Maclellan would have been surprised to be told that in under 200 years, his splendid new castle would lie a roofless ruin with the town languishing in economic slump. Daniel Defoe, visiting Kirkcudbright in 1724, said: 'Here is a harbour without ships, a port without trade, a fishery without nets, a people without business ... and though there is extraordinary salmon fishing, the salmon come and offer themselves and go again, and cannot obtain the privilege of being made useful to mankind.' The period of economic decline ended in the latter half of the eighteenth century when Kirkcudbright

The Tolbooth with market cross and detail of jougs at Tolbooth steps

shared in the growing prosperity which was spreading slowly across Scotland.

Besides Maclellan's Castle, the Tolbooth is an interesting survivor of the medieval period. Like most tolbooths, the tower and spire are given special attention by the building's designer. Erected in 1580, the Tolbooth has a three-stage tower with central spire and smaller corner spires. It tells you by architectural means that it is a building of importance, and overlooks the market square in much the same way that Glasgow's City Chambers broods over George Square. Public building and public square share a common relationship in much European town planning, no matter what the century.

The Tolbooth was the point where local taxes were paid, where burgh administration was carried out and where wrongdoers were imprisoned. The flight of stone steps and raised platform outside the Tolbooth door was used as the place from which to make public pronouncements. It was here that offenders were held in public chastisement and the jougs or iron manacles which held the prisoner secure are still in position.

On top of the steps stands the mercat cross, having been moved here in the nineteenth century from a position just north of the Tolbooth. The cross, dated 1610, has a triangular head set on a tall stone shaft. The original base of the mercat cross now supports a lamp standard; mercantile display has given way to public utility. The public water fountain is positioned in the wall of the steps and carries a plaque commemorating the bringing of water to the town in 1763. It says:

'This fount not riches life supplies
And gives what nature here denies
Prosperity must surely bless
Saint Cuthbert's sons who purchased this.'

The Tolbooth is said to have been built using stone from Dundrennan Abbey, a building where Mary, Queen of Scots spent her last night in Scotland. Dundrennan was destroyed at the Reformation when its lands were acquired by the Crown. Like Maclellan's Castle, the Tolbooth is built of other buildings' ancient stones. Some of these can be seen in the arch above the ground-floor doorway and in the spire.

Growth and prosperity have come to Kirkcudbright every 300 years or so, lasting for maybe 100 years and slowly declining. The ridges and troughs are like the local landscapes, but in terms of town growth it means that we need to look to the ridges to find periods that shaped the town. After the early settlement of the ninth century, the castle building of the twelfth century, the construction of the Tolbooth and Maclellan town house of the sixteenth century, we enter a new period of growth and change in the eighteenth century.

As in the previous periods of growth, Kirkcudbright is simply a small town caught up in bigger, often national, issues. First it was the Viking colonisation, then the imposition of crown rule, then the dissolution of the monasteries, and finally the Age of Enlightenment.

In the eighteenth century, the Scottish Enlightenment was ahead of much of Europe. The political economist Adam Smith, the architect Robert Adam, the moral philosopher David Hume, were the outstanding men of an outstanding period – visionaries and arbiters of taste. It was a period of great change in Scotland, when the countryside was planted up with hedgerows and ornamental woods, when the towns were given new straight streets, squares and grand terraces. From Kirkcudbright to Thurso, the new fashion for town planning quickly caught on.

New towns were all the rage in the eighteenth century – either as complete new communities like Inveraray in Argyllshire or as planned extensions to existing towns, like in Edinburgh. In the case of Kirkcudbright, the new town was built as an expansion of existing streets, forming a new planned town within the dog-leg of the old High Street.

Eighteenth-century 'New Towns' were often created by enlightened landowners, men who were well versed in the latest techniques and theories of design. The Earl of Selkirk, a relative of the Duke of Hamilton, was responsible for Kirkcudbright's new town as well as extensive woodland planting around the town. His tree planting was of sufficient fame to be mentioned in the *Statistical Account of Scotland* of 1794: 'The Earl of Selkirk has planted, with great taste and judgment, several hundred acres with various kinds of forest trees, such as oaks, beeches, ashes ... From the various improvements already made and still carrying on, the face on the country will, in the course of a few years, be totally changed. The most charming landscapes will strike the eye, and afford delightful subjects for the poet's fancy, and the painter's pencil.'

His son, the 5th Earl of Selkirk, had little hand in shaping Kirkcudbright, although perhaps inspired by his father's passion for town and estate improvement, set about opening up Canada. His activities were concentrated in the Red River area of Manitoba where he had extensive interests in the fur trade and then farming. He did much to help settle landless Scots who were forced off their land by the Highland clearances, establishing colonies first on Prince Edward Island and later more extensively in Manitoba. Born on Kirkcudbright's St Mary's Isle in 1771, he died in relative poverty in 1820, having lost much money in the collapsing Hudson's Bay Company. But his early settlement along the Red River became Winnipeg, the Provincial Capital, and nearby there is still a town called Selkirk.

The New Town, created by the 4th Earl,

A double bow-fronted Georgian house in High Street

A Georgian house in Castle Street built according to the Earl of Selkirk's feu conditions

consisted of four new streets – Castle Street, Union Street, St Cuthbert Street and St Mary Street – laid out to form a grid enclosed by the old dog-legged High Street. Rows of regular Georgian houses lined the new streets – regular but not identical. The houses were individually designed, not arranged as in some new towns as parts in a bigger palace-type frontage. This pattern of controlled individuality is further enhanced by different paint treatments and slightly differing doorway and window details. It provides a degree of variety along what could otherwise have become rather dreary streets.

In urban design, you have to strike a balance between order and variety, between solid and void, and between detail and the whole. In eighteenth-century Kirkcudbright, the balances are perfectly struck; the new streets

do not compete with the old and both Tolbooth and Castle still dominate the skyline. Clear skylines where public buildings and ancient spires rise above private rooftops suggest a town with civilised rather than commercial values. Kirkcudbright is one such town.

There are many eighteenth-century houses of note in the town and a handful of interest from the seventeenth century. The seventeenth century marks the end of the period of the local builder using well-tried traditional methods. The eighteenth century brings us to the world of professional designers – architects and engineers who had travelled widely, were well-read and rode around in coaches. It has often been said that to appreciate the architecture of the eighteenth century, you need to have an eye for proportion. Buildings of this period tend to be rather plain, almost severe, yet they always have harmonious proportions, a sense of symmetry and sometimes refinement and elegance of detail.

Most Georgian houses in Kirkcudbright are two storeys high and face directly onto the street. Although no two houses are exactly the same, there is a consistency of size and of finish which gives the street a sense of order in townscape terms. This consistency was achieved by attaching legally binding conditions on building as part of the sale of the ground. Known as feu dispositions, they allowed the superior – in this case the Earl of Selkirk – to protect and promote high standards of design and construction without being involved directly in the development. It was, in some senses, an early form of planning control where permission to build was granted, subject to conditions. The collective order and beauty of much of Scotland's urban architecture from the Georgian period onwards was achieved by such simple means.

A typical feu disposition in Kirkcudbright is one issued by the Earl of Selkirk to John Maclellan, merchant, in 1793. It applied to a building plot in Castle Street and amongst many conditions stipulated:

'... *good dwelling houses along the whole front of the street ... not under two storeys high making a height of eighteen feet ... built with a pavilion roof so that none of them have gavels (gables) to the street ... That these houses shall be covered and always kept covered with slates or metal ... and have none other than sash windows ... and the sides and lintels of windows and doors shall be built of freestone or granite ... that there shall be no forestairs ...*'

Castle Street has rows of fairly modest Georgian houses, some with shops, but all sharing excellent proportions and many painted in delightful fashion. The use of bright colours, often oil-based with a corresponding depth of colour, makes Kirkcudbright immediately enjoyable. Freshly rain-washed with a low bright sun, the effect is most attractive, recalling the mosaics of colour beloved by the Glasgow painters who settled in Kirkcudbright at the turn of the last century.

Rectangular grids of streets were a fashionable form of development in the eighteenth century. Much of Glasgow's urban grid dates from this period as do the gridded cities of the New World. Thomas Jefferson, American President and architect, called the grid the social equaliser, since it gave everybody equal rights. But in design terms, the grid imposes a respect for collective order and gives the relationship between buildings and street an added importance.

Grids are particularly vulnerable at the corners of street blocks. At corners, the visual frame of development should be tight and ordered but it is often destroyed by later development. In Kirkcudbright, such a break occurs at the junction of High Street and Castle Street where several older houses were demolished to build policemen's houses. The enclosure of space by building mass has been lost, what was once solid street architecture is now a collection of underscaled brick cottages. The retention of the former marriage stone of 1666 in one house hardly compensates for the loss of urban character.

Some of the Georgian town houses in Kirkcudbright stand comparison with the best in Scotland. Broughton House is a particularly fine example of a Georgian house which is far from provincial in appearance. It is set back from the High Street with a courtyard in front enclosed by wrought-iron railings. Once the town house of the Murrays, it is better known today as the home of the artist Edward Hornel. Broughton House is really a mansion house built in a town. Its ingredients of wide front with the central section given a pediment for emphasis speaks the language of the country house.

Edward Hornel lived here for much of his life. In that time, he built a large gallery and

Broughton House, home of the painter Edward Hornel

studio extension and, after spending eighteen months in Japan with his painter friend George Henry in 1893–4, he created a Japanese garden at the back. The magnolias, lily pond, stepping stones and creeping pines are straight out of an oriental garden. Things Japanese became very fashionable in artistic circles in the late nineteenth century – a fashion fanned by Whistler's paintings.

During Hornel's occupation of Broughton House, he commissioned the Glasgow architect, John Keppie, to carry out a number of alterations. These included the construction of a studio and gallery in 1909 which gave Keppie, a friend and partner of Charles Rennie Mackintosh, the chance to bring some Glasgow Style down to Kirkcudbright. Keppie designed an elaborate chimney-piece with a panel in relief of Scottish children playing pipes, and placed around the gallery a deep plaster frieze imitating the Elgin Marbles.

The whole gallery was top lit – a superb space to display the works of a successful painter. The gallery is typical of the design mood of the day when architects felt at liberty to borrow styles from anywhere, mixing Scottish with classical themes. The only surprise is to find no oriental references. Perhaps Keppie thought the spirit of Japan was best expressed in the garden.

Hornel's paintings are a rich patchwork of colour and draw their inspiration from the landscapes, legends and mysticism of Scotland. The colour harmonies of his paintings are somehow echoed in the colouring of the Kirkcudbright houses – bright colours in cheerful patterns.

Another artist who settled in Kirkcudbright at about the same time is Jessie King. A woman of considerable talent and enormous energy, she had a particular concern for Scotland's ancient architecture. She is best known for her book illustrations where knights in armour and willowy damsels wander around Art Nouveau landscapes. Like Hornel, she was inspired by the scenery around her, its woodlands and

81

The mosaic panel at 46 High Street. Right: Greengate Close, home of Jessie King

wild flowers, its old buildings and legends. Much of her decoration is drawn from local sources, the carvings on ancient rocks, but much is also drawn from her rich imagination. Jessie King's work is indelibly 'Glasgow Style'. She was one of the Mackintosh circle, and it was she who decorated the manuscript on the history of the Glasgow School of Art which lies buried beneath the foundation stone of Mackintosh's Art School building in Glasgow.

King lived and worked with her husband, E. A. Taylor, at 46 High Street, in a house known as Greengate. The mosaic panel over the close entrance marks the spot – a touching and quite Glasgow-Style way of doing things. Jessie King sought to make us aware of the artistic, rather than simply historic, value of our old towns. In 1934, she published an attractively illustrated book, *Kirkcudbright – A Royal Burgh*. It gives us a lasting record of the town fifty years ago – drawings of buildings now lost, of closes and streets whose cobbled surfaces have sadly disappeared under a sea of tarmac.

She starts the book: 'Kirkcudbright is attractive for its beautiful woods and flowers but there is another beauty, that of its old world buildings and closes ... It seems a pity that the charm of the outsides of these houses cannot be retained with the interiors re-modelled ... Perhaps it is only the hand of the artist that can save for the future the beauty in danger of being demolished and it lies with the fraternity to see that the romance of this old world town set in her historic stones, does not become entirely a thing of the past.'

Jessie King was warning against the demolition of historic buildings, a threat quite real in the 1920s and 1930s. She ends her book by illustrating old but crumbling properties at the corner of High Street and Castle Street which were eventually destroyed to make way for the police houses presently occupying the site. Of these old cottages, two features were rescued: the marriage stone which was built into the new houses, and the bow windows which Jessie King had built into her own house around the corner.

Splendid Georgian details are to be found and enjoyed all round the town: elaborate doorways, bow-front houses, flagged courtyards, decorative railings and attractive fanlights. It is the details which make up historic towns – without the rich texture of traditional details an old town becomes lifeless.

Considerable effort was put into composing house elevations along the new town streets. There was usually a centrally-placed door and one or two windows on either side with the pattern repeating above. These large Georgian houses, some the town houses of wealthy families with large rural estates, are one of the attractive features of the town. But the everyday architecture of the town is made up of more humble eighteenth-century houses, often only one or two rooms wide as against the three or four of the wealthy. To compose these cottages into elegant town houses, a clever trick was used of linking the front doors together, placing them under a single pediment, and arranging the single rooms on either side. The result was to produce attractive Georgian houses, whose rather grand appearance far exceeded the accommodation within.

Many of the principal town houses, especially in the High Street, use rusticated quoins at the edges of the main elevation. These big blocks of masonry are often placed two or three inches forward of the face of the wall, providing a kind of picture frame for the front elevation. Lesser streets use the same device but for the edges of the whole street rather than the individual building. In Castle Gardens, for instance, a row of eight slightly different houses is framed around rusticated quoins at either end. The quoins, often picked out in a different colour to that of the adjoining wall, define the corners of streets and provide a sharpness in visual terms to the rectangular town layouts.

A sense of places is established by architecture and urban design. Towns invested with a

great deal of architectural energy tend to be invigorating places to live – look at Milton Keynes as against Croydon or Bath as against Bathgate. Time and space are important ingredients and give rise to visual richness and historical layering. Townscape is a term we use to describe the collective character of towns: it looks at towns as an aesthetic experience, where buildings, streets and squares are all part of the overall scene much as fields and hedgerows are part of the visual world of the countryside. Because townscape deals with the collective view, the relationship between the parts takes on a special importance. Sometimes the whole town has a cumulative effect that is stronger than the sum of the individual parts – Kirkcudbright is that sort of town.

One of the few disappointing areas of Kirkcudbright is the patch of untidy land between the harbour and the town. John Wood's town map, prepared in 1824, shows that the old harbour once extended nearly up to St Cuthbert's Street. It was a rectangular basin formed in the Middle Ages and the town records refer to harbour repairs as early as the first half of the seventeenth century. This area has now been filled in and is used as a car park with the modern tourist information office sitting on what was, for centuries, the open water of the harbour. The important relationship between town and harbour has now been lost.

The character of a town is maintained by preserving old buildings, both the monuments and the more modest houses, and by designing new ones in sympathy with the values of the old. Keeping old buildings in use often requires periodic minor adaptation or a complete change of use to serve a new function. Old buildings were generally built to last and endure longer than the actual uses for which they were originally constructed. Hence the need for re-use, which is the key to successful conservation.

Kirkcudbright has several examples of recycled buildings now performing new roles – roles which the original builders would prob-

Left: a Georgian doorway in High Street

85

ably never have contemplated. Just west of Moat Brae are a group of rubble warehouses from the eighteenth century. These have now been converted into flats affording excellent views over the Dee. A particularly refreshing feature of the conversion is that the modern mason has signed and dated his work – expressing a sense of pride in his craft and leaving a record in stone for future historians.

Towns are a cultural and aesthetic resource which require careful management and planning, historic towns doubly so. Kirkcudbright has luckily escaped the wave of demolition that plagued the 1960s and is far enough away from big cities not to have been over-gentrified. By good fortune and relative isolation, it is a remarkably complete town of the seventeenth and eighteenth centuries.

A view of High Street

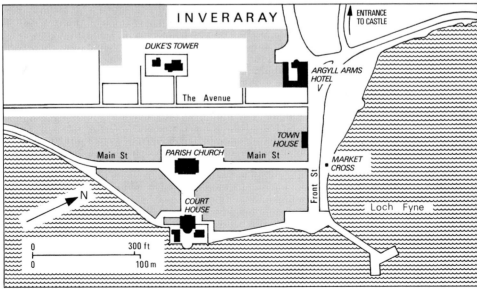

Aerial view of Inveraray

INVERARAY

Few towns sit more comfortably in the Scottish landscape than Inveraray. It manages, by conscious design, to exploit a wonderful loch-shore site. As if moved by the magic of the water's edge and the grandeur of the Highland scenery, those responsible for the new town of Inveraray excelled themselves.

To approach Inveraray along the old military road – the present A83 – is to move through a landscape which earlier generations would have called sublime. The first glimpse of the town, perhaps from Aray Bridge, a fine humpback bridge designed in 1775, is of a low white town sitting at sea level on a flat peninsula jutting into the loch. It was really an ideal site for a town: level, sheltered and with the makings of a good harbour.

The excellence of the town design is all the more remarkable for the comparative remoteness and inaccessibility of the site. Here two hundred years ago, with the help of some of the greatest designers of the age, the Duke of Argyll created not just a famous castle, but a new town and a huge landscape park. It was, in effect, the Versailles of the Highlands.

The town of Inveraray is perhaps the most imaginative and complete of the 120 or so brand-new towns and villages created in Scotland in the eighteenth century. New towns were very much a Scottish fad in the Georgian period and were part of a wider improvement movement which embraced agriculture and industry. For many Scottish landowners, the eighteenth century was a time to introduce onto their estates some of the new ideas on farming and forestry which had been tried out in the south. Shelter belts were planted, fields drained and enclosed, roads and bridges built and many new towns and villages created.

Scotland tended to embark on a new town and new village building boom, fifty to a hundred years before England. This is partly because Scotland never really had villages in the English sense. Centuries of civil unrest and the poverty of much of the countryside prevented the development in Scotland of a pattern of rural villages common to much of Europe. Consequently, most of the Scottish new towns were associated with agricultural or fisheries improvement – rather than being developed as industrial communities which was the pattern in the south. For this reason, Scottish new towns tend to have a formal Georgian character of straight streets and the occasional geometric square, rather than the irregularity of the English picturesque village. If parallels are to be drawn between new towns in Scotland and elsewhere, the closest comparisons are the new communities established on the eastern seaboard of North America. Here the right-angled grid of streets, the use of tenement blocks for housing, and churches placed in the centre of public squares, all show the debt urban America owes to eighteenth-century Scotland.

The building of the new town of Inveraray was a direct consequence of the building of the present castle. When the 3rd Duke of Argyll decided in 1744 to demolish his largely decrepit medieval castle and build anew, it involved the demolition of the collection of old houses huddled nearby. These old cottages, mostly single-storey and roofed in heather thatch, are recorded in John Clerk's painting of 1760. It was typical of the age to disregard the value of old buildings. The eighteenth century, like much of the twentieth, was concerned more with progress than conservation.

Inveraray from Loch Fyne

The new town of Inveraray was, therefore, the result of the building of the present castle. In this respect, its history is rather similar to the planned town of Fochabers in Morayshire where a new village was created in 1776 because extensions to Gordon Castle meant the destruction of the old village. This elegant town, not dissimilar in layout to Inveraray, was designed by John Baxter, who was for many years William Adam's master mason. The Adam family, father and sons, figure largely in the building of Inveraray.

Inveraray Castle, like the making of the new town itself, is the product of a number of differ-ent architects, often working in succession to each other and sometimes for different clients. The present unity in castle, landscape and town is a measure of the respect each designer held for the work of others. Of course, the Georgian style was a great unifier even when it was given 'Gothic' fancy dress, and the present estate, including the town, is a tribute to collective aesthetic ideals.

The three architects mainly responsible for the building of the Castle were the London architect Roger Morris who prepared the mas-ter plans in 1745, Robert Mylne who designed most of the interiors, and the eminent Scottish

architect William Adam who supervised the work. It took forty years to complete the castle, although its present appearance with tall conical roofs and gabled dormer windows in the Baronial style is the result of Victorian additions made a hundred years later. Though William Adam was brought in originally as Clerk of Works, the influence of the Adam family grew over the years, especially that of the elder son John who inherited William's practice on his father's death in 1748.

The Adam family, father and sons, was surely Scotland's most gifted family of architects and designers. Like all men of genius, their talents spanned many fields. William was a noted horticulturalist and garden designer, as well as architect; John too was a great tree planter and builder of Palladian mansions, and Robert, probably the greatest of all the Adams, a gifted artist, antiquarian and designer of interiors and furniture. All three – William, John and Robert – had a hand in fashioning Inveraray and to some extent, Inveraray fashioned them. Robert, employed at Inveraray Castle at the tender age of twenty, went on to design great 'Gothic' mansions such as Culzean Castle in Ayrshire which has more than a hint of Inveraray's castle style.

Above: Inveraray Castle. Right: William Adam's new town plan of 1747

Like Culzean Castle, Inveraray is best viewed as a classical mansion house with Gothic details, rather than a real Scottish castle, which it obviously is not. Neither is it a Gothic Revival country house in the picturesque nineteenth-century style of, say, Abbotsford. Instead, it is a symmetrical Georgian Palace, built with all the grandeur money could buy and clothed, incongruously some observers said, in Gothic fancy dress.

Between the Adams and Roger Morris, there stood another influential architect, Robert Mylne. Mylne was a distinguished member of a long line of Scottish master masons who had served the Kings of Scotland since the fifteenth century. Mylne's job was to supply the details of Morris's master design for the castle and to advise on other works, including the layout of the new town of Inveraray.

There is a tantalising lack of documentary evidence to establish the authorship of the design of new Inveraray, as the planned town was sometimes called. As early as 1747, William Adam had proposed a layout for the new town which had a central church built within a square with a main street orientated north-south focusing on a Tolbooth and placed roughly parallel to the shore of Loch Fyne. Adam proposed two designs, one with bastions which reflected the need for defence after the uprising of 1745, and one without. Adam's involvement at Fort George near Inverness had established him as an architect of military works – a talent he was clearly intent upon showing off to the influential Duke of Argyll.

Although William Adam's plan was not implemented, he planted the seeds of an idea which was adopted by others. This included the centrally placed church and a main north-south street placed parallel to an existing avenue of trees, known originally as the Mall. In the event, development started not in the centre of the town but at the east side facing the castle. Here John Adam had designed, in 1750, a number of public buildings including the Inn (the Argyll Arms Hotel), the Town House and a number of adjoining private houses. John Adam's plans for the new town were strongly influenced by his father's proposals but by 1770 there was still a wide gap between the grand conception and the reality of built development. This gap was eventually filled by Robert Mylne.

Even as late as the 1770s, with the castle practically complete, much of the old town still survived. It stood embarrassingly on the doorstep of the new castle and when the 5th Duke succeeded in 1770 he shifted the priority, in terms of finance and design talent, into completing the new town. It was the 5th Duke who employed Robert Mylne to enlarge upon Adam's earlier proposals and create a modern

town of industry and local commerce to house his estate workers. The Duke founded a woollen mill to spin the wool from the new breeds of sheep then being successfully introduced into the Highlands and encouraged the herring industry by building a new pier. With a mixture of eighteenth-century philanthropy and self-interest, the Duke was able to clear away the ugly old cottages surrounding his new castle and encourage the economic development of this remote Highland area.

It must be remembered that to create Inveraray – castle, new town and landscape – took considerable vision and no less considerable power. It was the age of grand gestures, particularly in architecture and engineering. What is especially remarkable about Inveraray is that all this was set in motion by a Duke who was then sixty-one years old, and in a landscape so remote that the nearest carriage road was forty miles away. What is more, successive Dukes spent only the summer months in Scotland, preferring high society and warm houses in or near London to the wind and rains of Scotland. Distance was both a problem and a

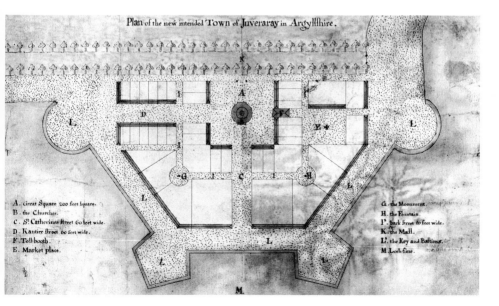

Plan of the new intended Town of Inveraray in Argyllshire.

A. Great Square 200 feet square.
B. the Churches.
C. St Catherines Street 60 feet wide.
D. Kantire Street 60 feet wide.
F. Tollbooth.
E. Market place.

G. the Monument.
H. the Fountain.
I. back Street 40 feet wide.
K. the Mall.
L. the Key and Bastions.
M Loch-fine.

benefit. For the Dukes, London provided contact with some of the best minds and greatest designers – like Vanbrugh whose original sketch influenced Morris. But distance led to delay and indecision, especially when countless intermediaries were involved. This was a problem for the creation of the new town rather than the castle or the park.

Mylne not only padded out John Adam's earlier town proposals, he also created unity and cohesion between the parts already built. Mylne achieved this by two clever means. Firstly, he built an arcaded wall to link together the separate buildings on Front Street and secondly, he built in a style which reflected the treatment of earlier buildings. The resulting town has a remarkable consistency of design, materials and layout – a consistency enhanced today by a unifying colour treatment. That Mylne should have achieved this in the face of delaý in implementing the Duke's proposals and with rival plans for the design of the new town already well established in some minds, is a measure of his skills. But Mylne was no second-rate architect, no mere provincial master of works based in Edinburgh. In 1758 he had won the architectural competition to design the new Blackfriars Bridge in London and, much to Robert Adam's chagrin, had at the age of twenty-five won the Papal Medal of St Luke's for architecture which was awarded in Rome at the Senatorial Palace on the Capitol. Robert Adam never really forgave Mylne his brilliance and viewed him as a dangerous rival, referring to him contemptuously by the nickname 'Blackfriars'.

The resulting town of Inveraray represents a coalition of talent of the highest order. The town remains not just one of the most elegantly designed of the new towns of eighteenth-century Britain but also one of the best preserved. Today it is a conservation area, and this helps preserve not only its overall character but also the countless details which make old towns so fascinating. Most of the individual buildings are listed as being of special architectural or historic interest and many of these are listed grade 'A' which reflects their national importance.

The town is arranged to be viewed from the north, on the approach which passes near the castle. Here, like a stage set composed along Front Street, the prospect of the town is seen to best advantage. The composition is designed about a major and a minor axis. The major axis is Main Street which runs at right angles to the bay and leads to the central square. About this axis are arranged two roughly symmetrical compositions, one on the seaward side of the street and the other on the landward. Each side consists of a main central house and two flanking houses. The main house on the landward side is a storey higher than its counterpart and is given a central pediment to reflect its importance.

The minor axis is The Avenue which runs for nearly a mile parallel to Main Street and is entered via an arcaded screen wall in Front Street. The Avenue originally marked the boundary between the town and the Duke's private park but is now open to the public. In the early days a high wall separated the town from the strictly private avenue and park and in this wall no doors were to be built, or windows unless under six inches wide.

The result of the major and minor axis and the formal compositions about them was to create a picturesque front to visitors who approached on the long and winding road from Glasgow. As all town roads and footpaths were kept as close as possible to the high-water mark, the first impressions were often rather watery ones, especially in storms. But on calm days at high tide the town could be delightfully reflected in the still waters of Loch Fyne, evoking a somewhat Venetian air, helped, perhaps accidentally, by Mylne's arcaded screen wall.

Now that the classical spire to the parish church has been removed, the only vertical accent to the town is the Duke's Tower, built as recently as 1923 as the belfry for the adjoining All Saints Episcopal Church. The tower with its quaintly-placed angle turret affords marvellous views of the town and Argyllshire landscapes but rather disrupts the formality of the town's original concept. At least the tower is placed well to the side of the composition and thankfully on the landward side where natural relief in the form of distant mountains and some ancient beech trees help mask the impact of the lanky intruder.

As we have already seen, Front Street was the first street to be developed and here John Adam's hand is at work. John, like brother Robert, was a master at decorating a rectangular box often divorcing outward appearance from internal function. His best building in Inveraray is undoubtedly the Town House, begun in 1755. Built like a three-storey classical mansion it strikes just the right balance between provincial good taste and the kind of sophistication reserved for patrons of note. Using familiar means of construction – harling and stone dressings – and an equally familiar language of architecture – pediments, projecting pavilions, rustication – Adam manages to squeeze a building of considerable refinement out of the rather modest brief.

The same refinement can hardly be claimed of the Argyll Arms Hotel, designed five years before. Here Adam has produced a nine-bay coaching inn with as much finesse as a barrack block. He seems to have relied over-much upon size and bulk to achieve a satisfactory solution, a design shortcoming not helped by the Victorian glass vestibule added to the front elevation.

The Argyll Arms Hotel cost over £1400 to build, a not inconsiderable sum in 1755, and this was paid entirely by the Duke. There was much delay in completing the Inn, mostly because building materials had to be brought some distance and because much of the available manpower was engaged upon the castle. In fact, over 600 workmen were employed at the castle at the time and this meant only a

Previous page: Front Street with John Adam's Town House. Above: the Argyll Arms Hotel

handful were free to build the Inn. But the main problem was the availability of building materials on the scale required. Over 6000 feet of timber had to be imported from Frederikstad in Norway and some 218,000 slates were cut at the quarries of Easdale.

The resulting Inn, finished in 1755 after four years on site, became a much-visited building. William and Dorothy Wordsworth stayed here as did Dr Johnson and James Boswell returning from their Hebridean journeys, and also a rather disgruntled Robert Burns. All three visits leave us with memorable quotes either of the Inn or the town. Dorothy Wordsworth said of the Inn that it appeared 'over rich in waiters and large rooms to be exactly to our taste, though quite in harmony with the neighbourhood'.

Dr Johnson said of the Duke of Argyll's work generally at Inveraray, 'What I admire here is the total defiance of expense.'

Robert Burns, feeling somewhat miffed by the quality of service, supposedly scored the following lines on one of the Inn windows:

'Who'er he be that sojourns here
I pity much his case,
Unless he comes to wait upon
The Lord their God his Grace.
There's naething here but Highland pride,
And Highland scab and hunger;
If providence has sent me here,
'Twas surely out of anger.'

Front Street is elaborately composed like the parts arranged on a proscenium stage. The composition is the result of Mylne's town front design dated 1786 which not only ties together the John Adam façades with a linking screen wall but turns the vital corner into Main Street.

Main Street, which was originally to be called Argyll Street, is really Mylne's creation. His design showed an entrance gateway to the Street but this was never built although a rather similar gateway known as the Northern Entrance was to the west of the Argyll Arms

Robert Mylne's Parish Church

Hotel. Main Street is the high point of Inveraray and shows the importance of urban design as a discipline quite distinct from architecture.

Urban design is concerned with the relationship between building mass and urban space. The façades of buildings take on a lesser importance, the primary concern is one of movement through space – that space being created by the solid blocks of buildings. Space in town design is, of course, occupied space – it is inhabited by people, cars, trees and public sculpture. The balance between the parts, between solid and void, between public and private, between plain and articulated is what urban design is really about. What Inveraray shows, albeit on a small scale, is that it is possible to plan a town from scratch and still achieve the right balance between formality of layout and quality of urban space.

Main Street opens at its mid-point to create a square, in the centre of which sits the very elegant double church of Inveraray Parish.

The church stands astride the cross axis on Main Street, the secondary axis of which is terminated by the imposing Court House built in 1820. Occupying the important focal point where the two streets cross, the Parish Church is given a location in the town which reflects the status of the building. As if in deference to the church, the road splits at this point to form a carriageway on either side of the building and about these roads the adjoining buildings are set back to form a square. Urban space is thus created, symbolic of function and ceremony, and if one can ignore the passing cars and tour buses, a place fit for a major public building. Mylne has responded to the site with admirable ease and his church rivals Adam's work in terms of urbanity and refinement.

It was not until 1795 that work began on the Parish Church and it was 1805 before the church was finished. Delay appears to be a prominent feature in the making of Inveraray; there were disagreements over the design (Mylne had suggested projecting porticoes at either side to serve as sheltered market stances), but the main problem was one of obtaining suitable materials. The local granite used for much of Inveraray was not considered of good enough quality for the finished stonework of the church and the Duke ordered that freestone from Arran be used. The result of the Duke's meddling in the design and taking issue over the materials proposed was to slow down the progress of work and ultimately produce a building of two colours of stone.

Nevertheless the final building is a success and although not built entirely as Mylne designed, it manages by good proportion and unusual application of classical details to look quite at home on its island setting. The use of Tuscan columns and Venetian windows recalls the architecture of Edinburgh's New Town which, in many ways, was a much bigger application of very similar ideas of urban design.

The interior of the Parish Church is full of surprises. It is a double church, one for English-speaking and one for Gaelic services, with a dividing wall of masonry right down the centre. Each church is entered at opposite ends of the building and each was originally galleried with staircases rising against the end walls. Over the centre of the church once stood a small classical steeple but this was removed in 1941, apparantly because it had become unsafe. The interior, pleasantly restored in 1952, has a Scottish Presbyterian air with its scrubbed pine and grey paint but the exquisite refinement of the joinery, for instance the Georgian bow doors, and the late Victorian pulpit in carved oak provide just the right level of detailed interest.

The axis which runs from the church at right angles to Main Street is terminated by another classical front, this time by the Edinburgh architect James Gillespie Graham. The building is the new Court House which was built after Adam's Town House became overcrowded. With its back to the sea and sheltered by a grim range of public jails and bastions thrusting out into the loch, the building's public front to the town square provides a façade of good Georgian manners to hide the horrors of penal servitude behind. Originally there were two jails – one for offenders and one for debtors – but these eventually became a prison for males and another for females. To prevent escape by sea, elaborate walls made of massive blocks of masonry were built along the headland. These prison buildings are presently disused but provide a rare opportunity to study the architecture of offenders before the introduction of more standardised prison buildings in the mid-nineteenth century.

Gillespie Graham's elevation facing the Parish Church seems to make more than a passing reference to Mylne's design. Like Mylne, Graham uses the Tuscan order and a central Venetian window but, with £5000 to spend, as against the latter's £1700, Graham could at least afford quality ashlar stonework for the whole of his front elevation. Some observers have noticed Robert Adam's influence in the design of the new Court House, for Graham was one of several architects a generation after Adam who fed off the great man's genius.

By describing the major buildings by John Adam, Robert Mylne and Gillespie Graham, I do not wish to give the impression that Inveraray consists solely of a townscape of monuments. Far from it, for the character and interest of the town is dependent more upon the collective order and consistency of lesser buildings than the individual contribution made by single ones. It is an order achieved partly by strict aesthetic controls attached to permission to build exercised by the laird and applied as binding conditions through the sale of feus, partly by the use of a relatively narrow range of building materials – mostly stone or harling for walls and slate for roofs – and partly by the practice in Scotland of building without front gardens, where the front elevation of the building forms the rear of the pavement. And, finally, by the use of compact forms of development, mostly tenement blocks or terraces.

All of these elements are present in the town of Inveraray and are the principal ingredients in the make-up of its urban character. Today's commitment to maintaining these traditions, largely through planning control which has, in many ways, taken over the Duke's former responsibilities regarding land use and amenity, means that the town enjoys a remarkable level of preservation.

A good street to illustrate collective order is Main Street. The street was developed over about thirty years and involved at least two different architects, although Mylne was mostly involved. The result is a very attractive street of black and white Georgian houses which achieve considerable order and dignity without the austere classicism of, say, the streets of Edinburgh's New Town. Each house in the street is painted white with black trim for windows, doors and quoins and, although no two houses are exactly the same, individuality takes second place to group effect.

To appreciate Georgian architecture, you need an eye for proportion. If you look closely at a Georgian façade you will notice a number of recurring proportions – the frontage is normally divided into two by a centrally placed door and split into two or more sub-bays. At the centre of each bay is placed a window, the proportions of which often correspond to the proportions of the bay division in which it occurs. The 'Golden Mean', a relationship of width and height of 5 to 8, is often used and it is sometimes applied horizontally to the building frontage and vertically to the windows. By these means harmony and repose are achieved with what often looks deceptively like little effort. In both Main Street and Front Street, you can see these proportions operating.

The effect of façade painting is to draw attention to the proportions – to underline an intention which may have been obscured by later additions or alterations. What often happens today, although thankfully but rarely in Inveraray, is that modern window replacements destroy the proportional harmony of an old building. Too often a slick aluminium window replaces a timber sliding sash to the detriment of the building's character.

Main Street is fortunate in still possessing many of its original windows and doors. It has also happily escaped the other great bugbear of historic towns – the modern shopfront and illuminated sign. Here the shops are discreetly designed and shop lettering is also well executed, either hand painted or made of cut-out letters painted black. These details of design are often overlooked today yet their cumulative effect is considerable in historic towns. Modern traffic signs can be a problem too and in Inveraray the highway authority has recently erected a road directional sign in Church Square whose scale and impact is more appropriate to a motorway. Nearly as bad, the overbright yellow parking lines introduce unwelcome splashes of colour in a town of white, grey and black.

Main Street rises up to the church at one end and frames an open view of the sea at the other. In the centre of the open view stands the mercat cross, moved here from the old town after suffering years of neglect. This venerable cross, dating from about 1400, shows that in spite of the 200-year-old new town, Inveraray is, in fact, an ancient settlement of some interest. As we have noted at Crail, the mercat cross was a symbol of burgh status, but it is clear from the design of the cross at Inveraray that its origins are ecclesiastical rather than secular. In fact, some historians have suggested that this ancient Celtic cross came originally from Iona and was brought here in about 1500.

The harbour has an interesting history. No trace of the old town harbour survives at the mouth of the Aray but the origins of the present harbour go back to 1754 when John Adam designed a pier for which he received a fee of ten shillings and sixpence (about 52p).

Adam's pier was considered too small for a growing town which, in 1795, is said to have

99

had a herring fleet of 500 boats. After much deliberation and delay Gillespie Graham was appointed to inspect the pier and make recommendations for its strengthening and extension. These were duly implemented, and it was further extended in 1836 with a grant of £800 provided by the British Fisheries Society, of which the 5th Duke was the first President.

The British Fisheries Society helped establish a number of coastal fishing towns in Scotland, including, amongst others, the west-coast towns of Tobermory, Ullapool and Oban. Formed in 1786, the Society's objective was to halt Highland emigration and to provide work

very close together and often arranged gable-end to the shore.

Inveraray pier today has become primarily a leisure pier catering for west-coast sailors rather than fishermen. It is, however, a marvellous example of a kind of robust engineering tradition reserved for working harboursides. Made of pink granite, yellow sandstone and grey whin, the various levels and function of different areas is usually marked by a change of material or a slight alteration to the tooling of the stone. Notice how the granite bollards are set into recesses in the pier walls to prevent collisions by carts trying to turn at the narrow jetty end.

A walk south along the headland towards the Court House takes us past Fern Point set behind garden lawns. Known originally as Richardson's House, it was the first private house built in the new town of Inveraray. It has two unusual features; a circular turnpike stair to the rear, and an orientation which is not parallel to either Main Street or Front Street. This example of non-alignment in a town of strict parallels is the result of its early date, 1752. At this time, ideas on town layout were influenced by William Adam's plan which proposed half an octagon of streets following roughly the line of the headland. So Fern Point was somewhat marooned artistically, caught between changes of taste or at least changes of Dukes, but it is a delightful house in its own right with a fine classical doorway of Doric columns, entablature and pediment, and an equally splendid garden wall with arrowhead railings.

The walk around the headland shows that behind the grand frontages and architectural showpieces, Inveraray is very much a working

and homes for crofters displaced during the clearances. The Society employed the engineer and planner Thomas Telford who designed the harbours and some of the housing layouts for these fishing new towns. Unlike Inveraray, the layout adopted, especially for exposed sites in the north, was of fishermen's cottages placed

Left: Gillies's House in Front Street with 'Golden Mean' proportions. Overleaf: Georgian doorways in Front Street and Fern Point

View of Main Street South with Arkland on the left and Relief Land on the right

town. Here we are in a land of tenements, warehouses and humble cottages. One of the plainest blocks is Relief Land on Main Street South. Built by Mylne in 1775, it lacks the stone window surrounds of the tenement opposite (Arkland 1774) – a weakness immediately evident upon entering the street. Mylne designed both sides of the street within a year of each other, but seems to have ignored the

fact that he gave the first block of building stone window surrounds when he gave the opposite block none at all.

The Duke apparently intended Relief Land to be plain, and certainly its name has a withering air. It was built to house the lowest class of workmen and constructed on the Duke's instruction of brick arches, rather than timber floors, in order to 'secure them from fire, a

well as to make the upper floor fit for such people, who would soon destroy any wooden floor'. As a result, a dreary harled block with not a detail to redeem it now stands opposite a row of fine tenements with the characteristic Inveraray pattern of black painted stone surrounds to doors and windows.

In spite of Relief Land, Inveraray – new town, castle and landscape – represents one of the high points of eighteenth-century design. It is a remarkable example of the Scottish Enlightenment, an achievement in architecture and town planning comparable, perhaps, to the great philosophical works of Adam Smith. In the relatively unvisited and remote Highlands, the Duke of Argyll created out of wilderness what is surely one of the most beautiful planned towns in Britain.

Aerial view of Rothesay

ROTHESAY

If the eighteenth century was the age of the spa, the nineteenth century was the age of the seaside resort. It was the Victorians who discovered the seaside, first for medicinal reasons – they thought the sea air and salt water healthy – and then for pleasure. If anywhere in Scotland sums up the Victorian attitude to the seaside, it is Rothesay. It was the perfect resort, complete with real medieval castle, and captures in buildings and layout the Victorian concept of holidays and pleasure.

A Victorian holiday to Rothesay required a journey by train and boat. Though only forty miles from Glasgow, getting to Rothesay involved a magical adventure where the train, the station, the steamer and the pier were all essential ingredients. Each stage of the journey had its own pleasure, its own mystery and its own rich imagery.

Not all journeys to Rothesay had to be taken via Wemyss Bay railway station, but for those that did, the experience was worth the effort. Built in 1903 by the Glasgow architect James Miller, the station has the grace and airiness of a palm house. Planned with curving platforms, curving concourse and circular booking hall, the building combines large areas of glass and the latest in structural engineering to create a railway station and steamboat terminus of distinction. The elegant lines, the touches of Art Nouveau, the web of open roof trusses all go together to make up a memorable interior. You are being told through architecture and engineering that the world of pleasure, beaches and dreams lies just across the water.

The nineteenth-century holiday was aided and abetted by the expanding network of railways and steamer services. They changed many a sleepy fishing town into a bustling centre of amusement and pleasure. Rothesay is a typical example – a small fishing burgh transformed into a thriving holiday resort in only a couple of generations.

The old town of Rothesay, which revolved around the magnificent thirteenth-century castle, was expanded first in the early nineteenth century. A ribbon of middle-class villas for wealthy Glasgow industrialists was built extending around the bay. All the new buildings faced the sea and most had big bay windows and verandahs to get the best possible view. By addressing its attention so noticeably to the bay, the seafront of Rothesay manages to achieve a visual consistency unusual for Scotland.

The ribbon of coastal development became reinforced during the Victorian period with hotels, guest-houses and tenements. The new buildings were built with public fronts which gave dignity, gaiety and coherence to the seafront. They seemed to recognise their collective responsibility in making Rothesay a special place – a kind of Glasgow by the sea, with all the sense of style and design consciousness that the city had in the nineteenth century.

Victorian Rothesay expanded both outwards and inwards from the old town, for many of the older buildings were removed by the nineteenth-century developers. Both seafront and castle grounds were respected by the Victorians and their town frames the old castle, forming hard edges of buildings around the ancient moat. The hilltops, too, were left wooded and free of development so that the three key elements in the character of Rothesay – sea, castle and landscape – were preserved. Sadly, the twentieth century has broken the landscape rule, houses now break the skyline and the rectangular bulk of Rothesay Academy juts out from the hillside.

To a seaside town, the harbour edge buildings are particularly important. They establish the division between town and working harbour and are usually the first buildings seen by visitors. At Rothesay, several terraces of elegant stuccoed houses face the harbour and Esplanade. Built usually four storeys high with plain or pedimented window surrounds and curved bays on all street corners, they give Rothesay an immediate sense of style. Recently painted in cream with chocolate and grey trim, the various terraces, all slightly different in treatment, have been unified by a thoughtful colour scheme. Against the mown grass and palm trees of the Esplanade, they look quite stunning, particularly in the morning sun shine.

It was Glasgow money that built Rothesay; money first from the middle class, later and of greater impact, the working class. Until the latter half of the nineteenth century, holidays

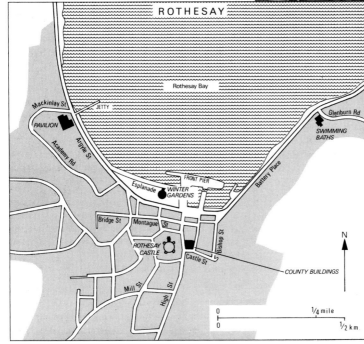

Above: interior of Wemyss Bay station James Miller, 1903

were the preserve of the middle class. The working class was given only Sundays and holy days off work and these were meant to be spent in church, certainly not enjoying yourself on the beach. It was only after Bank Holidays were introduced in the 1870s that day trips for leisure purposes became commonplace and these eventually led to the annual family holiday – 'doon the watter'. The money which the working class spent in Rothesay had been earned by hard graft throughout the rest of the year in the shipyards of the Clyde.

The middle-class holiday laid the foundations for the mass appeal of Rothesay in the early twentieth century. The Victorian holiday was generally a grand affair for those who

George Washington Wilson's view of the harbour c. 1880

A view of Rothesay bay

could afford it where the whole family, including grandparents and servants, booked into a large hotel for a week or two. Queen Victoria and Prince Albert set the fashion for quiet island holidays, preferring peace and seclusion at the Isle of Wight to high society in Brighton. Rothesay had much to offer which the discerning middle classes valued – an attractive beach full of seaweeds, classy hotels, an ancient castle and a wide Esplanade to spread the children out on.

The beach was always the centre of resort life. Without a good sandy beach, a Victorian resort was second class. Peopled by families, bathing machines and donkeys, the beach was the point around which the Victorian holiday revolved. It was also a place of scientific discovery. The nineteenth century was the age of collecting and classifying – fossils, animal life, shells and seaweeds all fascinated the Victorians. At the beach, families would gather and study seaweeds, referring perhaps to Mrs Gatty's book *British Seaweeds*. Seaweeds would

be taken back to the hotel for a closer examination and finally pressed or drawn. Queen Victoria was an avid seaweed collector and her interest helped make the hobby respectable.

The cult of the seashore as natural history led to the building of aquariums at a number of seaside resorts, including Rothesay. The aquarium was the marine equivalent of the Victorian palm house, a place where exotic or even frightening specimens could be peered at when it was raining outside. As the craze for aquariums waned in the twentieth century many were either demolished or converted to public baths. Today, the old aquarium at Rothesay is a swimming pool, populated by humans rather than octopuses or electric eels but the former splendour of the place survives.

In 1907, the aquarium at Rothesay, by then some thirty years old, had fallen on hard times. It was acquired by the Marquis of Bute who arranged for the Bute Natural History Society to use the halls, which now replaced the aquarium as a museum. A few years later it

George Washington Wilson's view of the aquarium c. 1890

was leased by a Mr McLeod, proprietor of the Glasgow Waxworks, as a general museum and musical hall. In 1933 the Bute Council, aware no doubt that the building faced closure yet again, recommended it be used as a public swimming bath and health pool. After substantial refitting and the reintroduction of the original sea-water element, it reopened in 1938 as the Rothesay Indoor Baths.

The baths were aimed particularly at the health resort market. The hot baths contained filtered sea-water and were particularly recommended as a cure for rheumatism. As the souvenir brochure of 1938 said: 'Warm sea-water baths, if skilfully given, are beneficial in a variety of cases.'

The Victorians were very conscious of anything to do with health – both public and private. Taking the sea air was one of the main excuses for visiting the seaside. Although the seaside always had some aesthetic appeal, a greater attraction was medical. Doctors advocated a spell by the sea, including even the drinking of sea-water as a cure for the great nineteenth-century epidemics of cholera or consumption.

Many a tombstone in places like Rothesay demonstrates the inadequacy of the seaside 'cure'. An example of such a tombstone stands just right of the gateway into the graveyard. It was erected by Thomas Bonnar, a wealthy Glasgow merchant, in memory of his youngest daughter Jean, who 'fell a victim to spasmodic cholera in eight hours severe affliction at Rothesay'. Another sad tombstone, this time erected by Angus McKay, stands in memory of his daughter Janet and 'ten of his children who died in youth'.

In the south, the Brighton Pavilion – the Prince Regent's holiday home – became the model for much seaside architecture. In Scotland, and particularly in Rothesay, it is the engineering tradition of the West of Scotland which tends to influence design and where decoration is required, it is frequently Art Nouveau. As a result, Rothesay is rather like

Victorian Glasgow by the sea – brash, enterprising and stylish. Rothesay was at the height of its prosperity between about 1890 and 1930. It was common for a Glasgow family to adopt a resort and return there year after year often staying at the same guest-house. Seaside resorts became great centres of entertainment: theatre, music hall and dancing. To accommodate these new entertainments, a new kind of architecture emerged at the beginning of the twentieth century – the Winter Gardens.

Winter Gardens were the Crystal Palaces of the seaside. Built of iron and glass, they usually featured the latest technology, creating huge barn-like structures with radiating girders and decorative iron castings. Rothesay Winter Gardens was prefabricated in Glasgow using Mac-Farlane Foundry Castings and floated down the Clyde in pieces and erected on the Esplanade. The MacFarlane Foundry made the parts for many a colonial building but this one reached only as far as the Isle of Bute. Similar castings can be found in places as far afield as India or Australia.

The Rothesay Winter Gardens was a meeting place in both high and low season. For the holiday-maker, it was a building to escape to in bad weather, a place to drink tea and Irn Bru amongst the palm trees and ferns. For the resident, it provided out-of-season enjoyment where Christmas pantomimes and pipe band concerts enlivened a long winter's evening.

Sadly, the building is now fairly dilapidated and although a listed building, the District Council tried to obtain consent to demolish it three years ago. Thankfully, better judgement prevailed and now a Building Preservation Trust has been formed by local people to restore the Winter Gardens and bring it back into holiday use.

The other public building to rival the Winter Gardens is the Pavilion built in 1938. Although it was constructed only fourteen years after the Winter Gardens, it looks like it hardly belongs to the same century. The Pavilion is modern, abstract and sleek. It shows the architectural revolution which occurred in the 1930s; a change in approach to design as well as in taste, which had spread into Britain from Europe and particularly Germany.

The Bauhaus School of Design in Germany in the 1930s had picked up ideas from the Cubist painters and the Expressionists and applied them to architecture and design. The Bauhaus is marked by an obsession with the geometry of primary forms – mostly cubes and circles and with bright colour. Decoration was eliminated and buildings were meant to be

Left: a melancholic tombstone in a Rothesay graveyard. Below: The Winter Gardens.

abstract designs whose appearance simply reflected their function. This was the beginning of what we now call the Modern Movement.

The Pavilion is designed to these strict principles by Ayr architect James Carrick who won a design competition for the building assessed by Thomas Tait. Tait had also been the assessor for the De La Warr Pavilion at Bexhill-on-Sea in Sussex and again awarded the design to a modernist architect, Eric Mendelsohn. German by birth, Mendelsohn was a brilliant Jewish architect who was chased out by the Nazis, and settled briefly in the United Kingdom and finally in America. The Bexhill Pavilion became a milestone of modern design and inspired the architects of the 1930s in Britain and abroad. Carrick, aware no doubt of Tait's fondness of modern design, based his competition entry on Mendelsohn's Pavilion at Bexhill. Naturally he won.

Bays and balconies are very much part of the character of Rothesay. They occur in many building types from detached villas and tenements to the splendid Pavilion. In the design of the Pavilion an enormous bow window is pushed forward thrusting out to sea. It was part of the language of modern architecture to play with the composition of building forms, to push cylinders through rectangles or thin walls through cubes.

At the Pavilion the projecting semicircular drum of the café is continuously glazed using curved glass set in metal window frames. Notice how the thin round columns which form the glazing line at the ground floor pass through the café interior and on to support the roof above. Plane, column and curve are combined with the same tension and sense of composition found in the paintings of the period.

Inside the Pavilion there are still many features of the original interior surviving. The auditorium is surrounded by rounded columns with swept tail-fin-like capitals, recalling the romance of early flying. The floor of the main staircase is another good example of 1930s' design. Here various colours of terrazzo –

Previous page: Rothesay Pavilion.

Above: Rothesay Pavilion interior designed in Bauhaus style

green, red, brown and white – are arranged in large abstract designs recalling the formal geometric paintings of Mondrian. Other period details can be found and, remarkably, have survived various upgradings over the years.

In Scotland, leisure piers never really caught on. Perhaps the severe winter climate discouraged even the most ambitious engineers from putting forward designs. Going for strolls along the pier was replaced in Scotland by walks along the Esplanade. The Esplanade in Rothesay is a wide pleasure land between the working town and the beach. It is here the crazy golf courses are to be found and the occasional paddling pool.

Rothesay is lucky to possess a splendid collection of seaside architecture along the Esplanade. Even the public lavatories enter into the spirit of the place. The gentlemen's lavatory by the harbour is as lavish as you are likely to find. This hall of convenience is arranged with a central island of urinals sharing a large common cistern with wall-mounted urinals and cubicles around the sides. The whole space is lit by a long ventilated rooflight which ensures copious supplies of that Victorian obsession – fresh air. The lavatories are floored throughout with mosaic which incorporates even the town's coat of arms. The walls are glazed with pink tiles below a green decorative cornice made of Doulton Ware. All the sanitary fittings are made by Twyford's Cliffe Vale Potteries and consist of green marbled ceramic ware. The designer of this public extravaganza even placed glass panels in the cisterns to display the flushing mechanism in all its glory.

Along the Esplanade, Art Nouveau crops up in the most unlikely places, like the fireplace in the ladies' toilet. As a style, Art Nouveau was a reaction against much of the Victorian taste for over-fussy decoration. It sought to simplify design using uncluttered patterns based often upon rather sensuous curves and soft colours. The style had its roots in continental Europe, where it was appropriately called the 'Liberty

The Art Nouveau pub interior in the Golfers' Bar

Style', but barely caught on in Britain with one major exception – Glasgow.

This city had a habit of going its own way in artistic terms and thanks to some exceptional art patrons and outstanding designers, produced some of the best Art Nouveau work outside Vienna. Naturally, the flowering in Glasgow led to a few seeds germinating down the Clyde and the Golfers' Bar in Rothesay is one of the results. The Golfers' Bar is typical, rather than exceptional, of the kind of Art Nouveau reserved for tearooms and pubs. Mirrors, stained glass and weird distortions of classical pediments are the details used to create interiors that are distinctly 'Glasgow Style'.

The everyday architecture of towns matters just as much as the set piece designs. Two Edwardian shopfronts are particularly worthy of attention. Built in Tower Street near the castle, they consist of black-painted joinery with gold and white lettering. Plate glass is counter-balanced by a row of small panes along the top of the shop window. The doors themselves are tall, narrow and multi-paned but in spite of the steepness of the street, the doorheads are kept at the same level. Above the shops are two flats reached by a central door with ornamental brackets on either side. The shops represent the kind of everyday design by anonymous builders once common in Scotland, but now sadly rare.

Besides the many later Victorian 'Glasgow Style' buildings, Rothesay has a number of earlier developments which give the resort a touch of class. Rockhill Castle is a good example of a villa made for a rich Clydeside industrialist. It is not, of course, a real castle; simply a splendid Victorian mansion house with plenty of turrets. Built in 1883, the villa was constructed for Ebenezer Kemp, one of a string of wealthy shipbuilders who were busy making themselves a fortune at the time. He had the misfortune to drown soon after the castle was completed in a sailing accident just offshore.

Brighton Terrace on Crichton Road

Rockhill Castle exploits the magnificent views to perfection. Terraces, bays and balconies are freely arranged to take advantage of the sea views and although the villa faces north, there are large full-height windows. Not all windows are clear glazed, for the villa uses stained glass with great enthusiasm. Each public room has at least one panel of coloured glass and these compensate for the lack of sunshine in the north-facing windows.

Nearby there is another interesting nineteenth-century villa. Known as Tor House, it was designed by the Glasgow architect, Alexander 'Greek' Thomson. He was a strong-minded architect who sought to transform the Greek Revival and make it into a dynamic modern style. Thomson was both architect and speculator – putting his own money into building developments. Usually Greek, but sometimes Egyptian or even Islamic, Thomson's buildings always stand out in a crowd.

There are several terraces of houses arranged in elaborate compositions facing the sea. Bay windows, gables and pretty dormers are carefully placed to produce symmetrical arrangements about a central point. It is only when viewed from the bay that these compositions become clear. Perhaps the designs were meant to be enjoyed by the passengers on the steamships entering the harbour. Brighton Terrace on Crichton Road is a good example and here the centre of the composition is marked by a carved stone nameplate.

With a view as stunning as that enjoyed across the bay from Rothesay, it is no surprise to find extensive areas of glass facing the sea. Tenements and villas, which elsewhere in Scotland would have been mostly solid sandstone walls with windows, are in Rothesay built mostly of glass with the minimum of structural support. Plate glass had become fairly cheap by the mid-nineteenth century and, combined with cast-iron construction, allowed the building of highly glazed walls. When used in combination with the fashion for bay windows, the effect of the iron and glass could be quite dramatic, as the tenement block known as Glenfaulds in Mount Stuart Road amply demonstrates.

The decorative tradition is part of seaside architecture. Cast iron allowed decoration to be mass-produced and it was possible to produce a building in iron, glass and stone capable of rivalling the carved timber architecture of, say, a San Francisco gingerbread house. There is much cast iron in Rothesay. It occurs in railings, lamp standards, columns and decorative downpipes. Decorative ironwork is used to embellish the severity of sandstone, to give it a prettiness in keeping with the seaside. The Grand Marine Hotel facing the Esplanade uses ironwork in this way.

Much of the ironwork in Rothesay comes from the great Glasgow ironfoundry of Walter MacFarlane and Co. One of the directors of the company was Thomas Russell, who for several years was Rothesay's Member of Parliament. He was responsible for several development schemes in the town, including the remodelling of Russell Street in 1870. Along the street he built an attractive block of tenements in the fashionable Scottish Baronial style and embellished the fronts with much decorative work – thistles and the like – some of it in iron. It was perhaps Russell's influence that led to the erection along the Esplanade of the splendid collection of cast-iron lamp standards. Individually numbered and attractively painted to pick out the town's coat of arms which are entwined amongst the foliage at the top, they add much pleasure to a stroll along the front.

The late nineteenth century was the period of the great seaside hotel. Looming above the seafront or set behind landscaped terraces, the big hotel reflected the wealth that was flowing into the seaside towns. Rothesay's Glenburn, built in 1890 and called originally the Glenburn Hydro-pathic, is the town's grandest hotel. Set high on a clifftop overlooking the bay, its symmetrical grandeur looks more akin to a stately home than a provincial hotel.

The Glenburn was designed by the Dumbarton architect John Crawford, who also designed ship interiors for the Clydeside shipbuilders William Denny and Brothers. Many of the Glasgow architects mixed building design with that of ship saloons and Crawford was one of the first to break into this lucrative market. The Glenburn was all that the grand seaside hotel stood for. It was lavish, expensive and exotic. Inside there were once Turkish baths, smoking rooms, marble floors and Persian carpets. The wealth of Glasgow, at the time the second city of the Empire, had found its way down the Clyde.

A class of building which saw a great boom at the seaside in the nineteenth century was the church. Religion had always followed in the tracks of holiday-makers, whether it was the Sunday School prayer meeting on the beach or formal worship in a church. Resorts

Decorative ironwork is a feature of Rothesay

soon found themselves building churches to accommodate the many different sects whose members flooded the seaside on their holidays, and such an appetite for building has left its mark upon the skyline of Rothesay.

The thirteenth-century castle has always made Rothesay special and was a great attraction to the Victorian holiday-makers. Its ruined walls have for centuries dominated the old part of the town and until fairly recently they had a picturesque covering of ivy. The Marquis of Bute – the owner of the land surrounding the town as well as many properties within it – paid for the castle's restoration in the 1880s. Today the old walls are consolidated and decay arrested but one regrets that the romance has been sacrificed at the expense of pointing and short-cropped grass.

Rothesay Castle was always a favourite Royal resort – the Kings Robert II, Robert III, James IV and James V all stayed here for extended periods. The association with royalty continues today although in title only. The Duke of Rothesay has remained since 1399 the heir to the Scots throne, and the title is now held by the present Prince of Wales.

Across from the castle stands the Bute County Buildings in a kind of fancy-dress castle style fashionable in the 1830s when it was built. Only an arrow shot away from the real thing, this fantasy of battlemented parapets and corner turrets was designed by the Greenock architect James Dempster. He had responded, no doubt, to the problem of designing a large public building in the shadow of the castle but unfortunately, the rigid symmetry of his design and the rather heavy-handed clock tower has produced a building with as much romance as a Victorian prison.

In the High Street above the castle stands the town house of the Marquis of Bute. It is a handsome example of seventeenth-century burgh architecture. For centuries the Marquis of Bute has shaped the town, controlling new development and fashioning the landscape of the surrounding hills. Mount Stuart, their principal residence, is only a few miles away, yet it was important for the Marquis to maintain a presence in the town. Recently restored, this old building is a model of how to treat an historic building.

By way of contrast, Presto's supermarket in Montague Street lies within the Rothesay Conservation Area. It is a building which seems to me to pay scant regard to the character of the rest of the street – a failing common to much modern architecture. What was once a street scene of tall vertical blocks of sandstone tenements and houses, has given way at this point to a low horizontal supermarket made of bricks. The enclosed lofty character of the street has been lost and the old building line, respected for centuries, ignored. Perhaps when the site is redeveloped, the traditional qualities of Scottish townscape will be reintroduced.

Rothesay could offer much to the Victorian holiday-maker. A wide Esplanade dotted with palm trees, a sandy beach, tearooms, ice-cream parlours, aquarium, and smack in the middle of the town, a real Scottish castle. For many a child, it must have been a fantasy world come true right down to the watery moat surrounding the castle. Before Disneyland and the movies, places like Rothesay were the dream worlds where the hard-working Clydesiders could escape.

But at the end of the day, the cult of sun worship was perhaps Rothesay's downfall. In the nineteenth century, the seaside was a place to go for health and later for pleasure. But in more recent times, the seaside holiday has become closely associated with sun tans. A good sun tan is seen as a sign of health and virility – good looks rather than health is the order of today. Unfortunately, Rothesay cannot guarantee a sunny week even in the height of the summer. But a sandy beach, a medieval castle, a priceless collection of seaside architecture more than compensate for a week in the rain.

Rothesay demonstrates one further lesson of town design – the importance of taste. Good taste is always desirable and Rothesay has many admirable examples, for instance the stuccoed terraces facing the Esplanade. But bad taste has its place too since it provides contrast and sometimes shock in the form of garish colour or new shapes and this can be seen in the 1930s' cinemas or modern amusement arcades. What cannot be defended or condoned is tastelessness, that all too familiar indifference to visual values. Give me good taste any day, bad taste sometimes, but tastelessness never.

INDEX

Page numbers in *italic* refer to the illustrations

Abbotsford, 16
Adam, John, 91, 93–6, 95, 99
Adam, Robert, 76, 91, 94, 95, 98
Adam, William, 90–3, 93, 101
Ailred of Rievaulx, 69–70
Albert, Prince Consort, 112
Andrew, St, 17
Anstruther, 55
Argyll, Dukes of, 89, 92–100, 104–5
Art Nouveau, 107, 113, 120–1, *120–1*

ba'game, Kirkwall, 33, 37
Balfour, Captain, 40
Ballachulish, 41
Bauhaus, 115–18
Baxter, John, 90
Beaton, Cardinal David, 20
Beaton, Archbishop James, 20
Bell, Andrew, 24
Bonnar, Thomas, 113, *114*
Boswell, James, 96
British Fisheries Society, 10, 100–1
brochs, 9, 35
Brodgar, Ring of, 35, *36–7*
burgh walls, 16
Burn, William, 24
Burns, Robert, 96
Bute, Marquis of, 112, 124–5

Caithness slates, 41
Carrick, James, 116–19, *118*
cast iron, Rothesay, 123, *124*
Castledykes, 69
Chalmers, MacGregor, 24
Clerk, John, 89
climate, 9, 33, 39

colour, building materials, 25, 69
Conolly, Daniel, 65
Constantine II, King, 67
courtyards, St Andrews, 18, 20
Crail, 9, 51–67; Castle Street, 55; Castle Terrace, 66, *66–7*; Custom House, 63, *64*; Friar's Court, *56–7*, 66; Golf Hotel, 63–5, 65; harbour, 61–3, *61*, *64*; High Street, 51, 54, 55; King Street, *54*; Kirk, 55, 58, 60; Kirkmay House, 66; market cross, 60–1; Marketgate, 51, 54, 55, *56–7*, 66, 67; Nethergate, 51; Priory Dovecot, 62, 63; St Mary, 58, *58*, *59*; Shoregate, 63; Tolbooth, 55, 58–60, *60*, 65
Crail Golf Society, 65
Crawford, John, 123
crow-stepped gables, 52–3
Culross, 51
Culzean Castle, 91–2
Cuthbert, St, 69

Defoe, Daniel, 75
Dempster, James, 124
Dundee, 30
Dundrennan Abbey, 76
Dunfermline Abbey, 43
Durham Cathedral, 43, 45
Dutch architecture, 25, 60

Easdale, 41, 96
East Neuk towns, 51, 53, 55
Edinburgh, 10, 13, 30, 39, 40, 76, 98, 99
Edward I, King of England, 69

Fergus, Lord of Galloway, 69, 74
Fife, 28, 51, 52
Fife Ness, 67
Flotta, 37
Fochabers, 90

Gatty, Mrs Margaret, 112
Glasgow, 10, 13, 46, 76, 79, 82, 107, 108, 115, 121, 123
Gledstunes, Herbert, 71
golf, 28–30, 65
Graham, James Gillespie, 98, 100

harbours, 10; Inverary, 99–101; Rothesay, 108, 110–11; St Andrews, 17, 28, 29
harling, 41, 52
Hope-Scott, James, 30
Hornel, Edward, 79–81, 80–1
Hume, David, 76

Innes, J. and G., 21–2
Inveraray, 9, 76, 89–105; Argyll Arms Hotel, 95–7, 95; Arkland, 104, 104; The Avenue, 94; Court House, 97, 98; Duke's Tower, 94–5; Fern Point, 101, 103; Front Street, 94, 95, 95, 96, 99, 100–2; harbour, 99–101; Inveraray Castle, 90–3, 92, 95; Main Street, 94, 96–7, 99, 104–5; mercat cross, 99; Parish Church, 97–8, 97; Relief Land, 104–5, 105; Town House, 95, 95, 98
ironwork, Rothesay, 123, 124
Isle of Man, 33
Isle of May, 61

James II, King of Scotland, 28
James IV, King of Scotland, 124
James V, King of Scotland, 124
James VI, King of Scotland, 15, 58, 60
Jefferson, Thomas, 79
Johnson, Dr Samuel, 96

Kemp, Ebenezer, 121
Kennedy, Bishop James, 18
Keppie, John, 81
King, Jessie, 81–2, 82, 83
Kirkcaldy, 10
Kirkcudbright, 10, 69–87; Broughton House, 79–81, 80–1; Castle Gardens, 85; Castle Street, 78, 78, 79, 82; High Street, 69, 71, 77, 78, 79, 82, 84, 85, 86–7; Maclellan's Castle, 71, 73, 74–6, 78; Meikle Yett, 69–71; mercat cross, 76; Moat Brae, 74, 87;

Old Greyfriar's Church, 71, 74; St Cuthbert Street, 78, 85; St Mary Street, 78; Tolbooth, 71, 75, 76, 78; Union Street, 78
Kirkwall, 9, 33–49; Albert Street, 38, 40; Bishop's Palace, 46, 48; Bridge Street, 39, 41–2; Broad Street, 37; Custom House, 40, 40; Earl's Palace, 46, 47, Girnell, 49; Harbour Street, 39, 49; Junction Road, 38–9; Kirkwall Hotel, 39; St Magnus Cathedral, 10, 33, 37, 42, 43–6, 43–5, 49; St Olaf, 33; Shore Street, 49; Spences Square, 40, 41; Tankerness House, 39–40, 39; Town Hall, 42–3; Victoria Street, 37, 40
Knox, John, 18–19

Linlithgow Palace, 16
lintels, 63, 64–5, 66
Lorimer, Robert, 10

MacFarlane Foundry, 115, 123
McKay, Angus, 113
Mackintosh, Charles Rennie, 10, 74, 81, 82
Maclellan, Sir Thomas, 74–5
Mary, Queen of Scots, 20, 76
Maxwell, Sir Robert, 74
Mendelsohn, Eric, 118
Miller, James, 107, 108–9
Morris, Roger, 90, 92, 94
Musselburgh, 60
Mylne, Robert, 90, 92–9, 97, 104
Myrton, Sir William, 58

National Trust for Scotland, 26
new towns, 76–9, 89, 92–4, 93
Norsemen, 10, 33–7, 45, 51, 69, 76

Orkneys, 33–49
Oswald, St, King of Northumbria, 69
Ottir, John, 63

pantiles, 28, 52
Patrick, Earl, 46
Peerie Sea, 37
Picts, 34, 39
pilgrims, St Andrews, 22

Reformation, 15, 16, 18, 24, 46, 58, 76

Regulus, St, 17
'rigs', 25, 55, 63, 71
Robert the Bruce, 58
Robert II, King of Scotland, 124
Robert III, King of Scotland, 18, 124
Rognvald, Earl, 33, 46
roofs, 10; Crail, 52–3, 53; Kirkwall, 40–1; St Andrews, 28
Rothesay, 10, 26, 107–25; Aquarium, 112–13, 113; Brighton Terrace, 122, 123; Bute County Buildings, 124; Castle, 124; Esplanade, 108, 120, 123, 125; Glenburn Hotel, 123; Golfers' Bar, 120–1, 121; harbour, 108, 110–11; Montague Street, 125; Pavilion, 115–20, 116–19; Rockhill Castle, 121–2; Russell Street, 123; Tor House, 122–3; Tower Street, 121; Wemyss Bay railway station, 107, 108–9; Winter Gardens, 115, 115
Royal and Ancient Golf Club, 28–30, 31
Ruskin, John, 69
Russell, Thomas, 123

St Andrews, 9, 11, 13–31, 51, 55; Abbey Walls, 16; Bishop's Castle, 17–18, 20, 28; Blackfriar's Chapel, 24; Cathedral, 13, 15, 16, 22, 24, 28; harbour, 17, 28, 29; Holy Trinity, 13, 24; Louden's Close, 27; Madras College, 24, 25; Market Street, 15, 22, 22; monastery, 16; North Street, 15, 22–4, 26, 28; Old Course, 28–30; The Pends, 16, 17, 25; St Leonard's College, 18, 20; St Mary's College, 18, 20, 20–1, 25; St Rule, 13, 16, 17; St Salvator's College, 13, 18–19, 19; The Scores, 19–20; South Street, 15, 15, 22–5; Town Hall, 24; university, 18–22, 19–21; West Port, 15, 16
St Andrews Preservation Trust, 26–8
sandstone, 53
Scott, Sir Walter, 16, 30, 46
Scottish Baronial style, 43, 74
Scottish Enlightenment, 76, 105
Selkirk, Earl of, 74, 77–8, 79
Skara Brae, 35–7
slate, 10, 41, 52
Slezer, John, 13, 14

Smith, Adam, 76, 105
spires, 55
Stavanger, 33
Stevenson, Robert, 10, 61
Stirling, 39
stone, 10; colour, 25; Crail, 51; harling, 41, 52; Kirkwall, 40, 43–6; re-using, 16–17, 41
Stromness, 39

Tait, Thomas, 118
Taylor, E. A., 82
Telford, Thomas, 10, 49, 101
Thomson, Alexander 'Greek', 122–3
Thorfinn, Earl, 34
tiles, pantiles, 28, 52
tourism, 11, 46
town planning, 9, 13–15, 22, 76–9, 89, 92–4
Trondheim, 45
Tucker, Thomas, 75

Vanbrugh, Sir John, 94
Victoria, Queen, 46, 112

walls, 10; burgh, 16; Crail, 54–5, 63; St Andrews, 20, 26
Wardlaw, Bishop Henry, 18
William the Old, Bishop, 46
Wilson, George Washington, 29, 43, 46, 61, 63, 110–11
windows, Rothesay, 123
Wordsworth, Dorothy, 96
Wordsworth, William, 96
wynds, 26, 33, 35, 51, 71

Picture Credits